SOAR ABOVE

SOAR ABOVE

How to Use the Most Profound Part of
Your Brain Under Any Kind of Stress

Steven Stosny, PhD

Health Communications, Inc.
Deerfield Beach, Florida

www.hcibooks.com

**Cataloging in Publication Information is available
from the Library of Congress.**

© 2016 Steven Stosny

ISBN-13: 978-07573-1908-2 (Paperback)
ISBN-10: 07573-1908-4 (Paperback)
ISBN-13: 978-07573-1909-9 (ePub)
ISBN-10: 07573-1909-2 (ePub)

Publisher: Health Communications, Inc.
      3201 S.W. 15th Street
      Deerfield Beach, FL 33442–8190

Cover design by Larissa Hise Henoch
Interior design and formatting by Lawna Patterson Oldfield

CONTENTS

PREFACE

This book began as a way of answering three questions that have nagged at me throughout my thirty-plus years of clinical practice:

- Why do so many smart and creative people make the same mistakes over and over, in life, work, and love?
- At what point does the unavoidable emotional pain of life become entirely avoidable suffering?
- How do we escape suffering while remaining vibrant and passionate about life?

Neurological discoveries in recent years have helped answer the first two questions, as we'll see in the body of the book. But the third question goes beyond science to the very nature of what it means to be human.

We're Animals, After All,
But Much More

The brains of all animals readily form conditioned responses to better negotiate the world around them. A rabbit nibbling on grass automatically runs when shadows move on the ground, even if it never witnessed a hawk swoop down on a littermate. The shadows are associated with an impulse to run, not necessarily with danger, when the moving shadows in its life experience were from branches of trees swaying in the breeze. Most of us will turn on an electrical device—TV, radio, smartphone—when coming home to an empty house or apartment, but not necessarily because we're lonely. Our brains have associated quiet in the home with an impulse to seek passive stimulation, lest we fall into stupor. We're less likely to reach for the electrical device when we come home engrossed in thought. The brain tends to associate interest with depth of learning or experience, rather than distraction, and with proactive, not passive, stimulation.

The human brain forms conditioned responses not merely to environmental cues, such as moving shadows, brewing storms, and quiet houses. Our brains build conditioned responses to physiological and emotional states, our own as well as those of others. A slight drop in blood sugar causes many people to fantasize about candy or ice cream. Many folks grow sad when tired. Many more look for someone to blame when they feel distressed for any reason. Almost everyone reacts automatically to the physiological signs and emotional displays of others. It feels as if they bring us down or rev us up, attract or repulse us, without a word being said.

The rabbit is probably better off running when shadows move on the ground. But the world we live in is much more complex than a backyard of thick grass, shady trees, and, on very rare occasions, shadows from a soaring hawk. The world we live in is fraught with nuance and ambiguity.

The Great Limitation

The brain strings together a series of conditioned responses to forge habits, which are behaviors that run on autopilot—things we do without thinking. As we'll see later in the book, much of what we do, we do by habit. More pointedly, habits rule under stress, when the mental resources required for intentional behavior are taxed. The extensive training for stressful jobs—from military service to air traffic control—is necessary to overcome the formidable limitations of conditioned responses and habits.

Habits limit growth and well-being because the two major regions of the human brain mature nearly a quarter century apart. Most of our conditioned emotional responses had been shaped into habits *before* the profound part of the brain—the upper prefrontal cortex—was fully online. We make the same mistakes again and again, even though we *know* better, because under stress the less sophisticated part of the brain overrides the ability to invoke most of what we've learned.

Many of the habits activated under stress violate our deeper values—for example, blaming, yelling, stonewalling, or devaluing loved ones. To escape the guilt, shame, and anxiety that are unavoidable in violating deeper values, we employ the prefrontal cortex, not to correct and regulate our toddler-like responses, but to *justify* them. Justifying behaviors that violate deeper values not only makes things worse, it greatly increases the likelihood of repeating the behavior. That's why we distrust people when they're defensive—they seem to be justifying violations of deeper values. Our experience tells us that justified behavior is likely to be repeated.

The great limitation of the human brain is its tendency under stress to engage complex social interactions—not to mention the complicated and nuanced emotional terrain of close relationships—with feelings and behaviors conditioned in the part of the brain dominated by "Mine" and "No." It's a tendency that we must rise above to reduce emotional pain and that we must *soar above* to achieve a life of meaning and purpose.

Soar Above

To soar above is to go beyond limits, to become greater, to become the most empowered and humane persons we can be. The ability to soar above the limitations of habits and conditioned responses is a large part of what it means to be human.

The goal of this book is to use habits to overcome the limitations of habits, that is, to forge habits of invoking the most profound part of the brain under stress. These new habits will transform us into the kind of persons, parents, and partners that, deep in our hearts, we most want to be.

CHAPTER 1

The Profound Brain

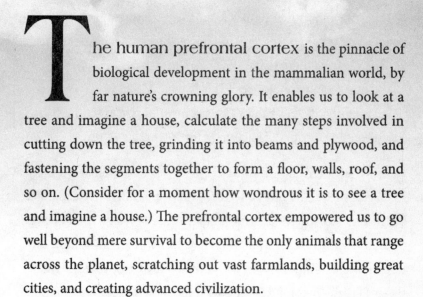

The human prefrontal cortex is the pinnacle of biological development in the mammalian world, by far nature's crowning glory. It enables us to look at a tree and imagine a house, calculate the many steps involved in cutting down the tree, grinding it into beams and plywood, and fastening the segments together to form a floor, walls, roof, and so on. (Consider for a moment how wondrous it is to see a tree and imagine a house.) The prefrontal cortex empowered us to go well beyond mere survival to become the only animals that range across the planet, scratching out vast farmlands, building great cities, and creating advanced civilization.

A relatively late addition to mammalian species, the prefrontal cortex (PFC) exhibits many specialties, including analysis, sensitivity to the perspectives of others, judgment, calculation, and regulation of impulses and emotions. It appraises environmental cues and organizes information to reconcile those appraisals with internal experience—thoughts, sensations, emotions, and impulses—in a process known as *reality-testing*. It then decides on behavior consistent with learned preferences, prejudices, or deeper values.

The strongest internal signals to which the PFC must apply reality-testing are emotions. Consistent regulation of emotions requires continually:

- Interpreting emotional signals (This is how I feel)
- Testing emotional signals against environmental cues (There is something or someone around me making me feel this way or there isn't; it's a false alarm)
- Considering preferences (This is what I like)
- Weighing deeper values (This is most important to me)
- Deciding a course of action (This is what I will do)

As I look out my office window, I feel a sense of peace within. My PFC tests the reality of that feeling and decides that it is accurate, because I'm looking at a beautiful lake lined by lush trees. I decide to linger with the splendid lake view. But if the reality were different—for example, there was a storm—my PFC would regulate the anticipated peaceful feeling with the more urgent information from the environment, and I would probably check the windows and ensure that nothing important is loose in the backyard. Or if the lake was peaceful, but I felt anxious or depressed when looking at it, the PFC would modulate my internal experience to match the beauty of the environmental cues, because reverence for natural beauty is a deep personal value of mine. In other words, I'd remove focus from my feelings, which would allow appreciation of my surroundings. As a result, I'd feel better.

The PFC provides a level of self-awareness and awareness of others unparalleled in the animal world by virtue of what psychologists call *theory of mind*. That's the ability to ascribe mental states, such as beliefs, feelings, motives, and desires, to self and others. Perhaps most important, the PFC enhances our most humane qualities, such as appreciation and higher order compassion—sympathy for vulnerabilities that we do not share. Thus we are able to create connections of value with other people, in which we both give and receive emotional support. As a byproduct of its combined processes, the PFC creates value and meaning in our lives.

Nature Saves the Best for Last

Not only did it develop late in evolutionary history, the PFC matures late in each individual due to delayed myelination, which isn't complete until the second decade of life. Myelin is the substance that lines nerve fibers to protect and insulate neurons. It aids in the quick and accurate transmission of electrical currents carrying data from one nerve cell to the next. In other words, the PFC isn't functionally "online" much before the second decade of life. Hence, it is called the *Adult brain*.

As we mature, the Adult brain gradually takes over dominance from that which controls the world of toddlers: the primitive limbic system, a relatively small region common to all mammals. (When you see a picture or model of the brain, you don't see the limbic system. The large cerebral cortex sits over it like a helmet with a slit in the middle, where the two major hemispheres of the brain join together.) Although the brain is always changing, the limbic system is pretty much fully developed on a structural level by age three. Hence, it is called the *Toddler brain*.

The primary survival function of the limbic system is to generate an alarm. But it has little reality-testing capability—that is, it can't distinguish what is really happening in the environment from what is being thought, imagined, or dreamed. That's how we can have intense emotions when nothing is happening around us, invoked by thoughts, memories, imagination, or dreams. Reality-testing is the province of the Adult brain.

From a survival standpoint, the gap in development between the Toddler brain and the regulatory Adult brain makes sense. The only way toddlers can survive is to sound an alarm that will get adults to take care of them. There is little survival advantage in regulating the alarm as long as the underdeveloped PFC is incapable of figuring out how to make things better. Because they can do very little for themselves, toddlers must manipulate their caregivers into doing things for them. Later in toddlerhood they're able to cajole with sweetness and affection. (What is more adorable than a three-year-old?) But early on they coerce caregivers through their greatest tool—the *alarm*, ranging from persistent whining to full-blown temper tantrums. (We tolerate the harshness of the alarm in toddlers because they're so damned cute and lovable.) When comforted instead of punished when they experience intense negative emotions, toddlers learn that they do not have to hide part of themselves to gain connection. When connection persists during positive and negative experience—that is, when caregivers do not react to the alarm either by rejecting or withdrawing affection—children learn gradually that they prefer the positive experience of the connection to their reflexive reaction of "No! Mine!" They begin the lifelong task of balancing the *Grand Human Contradiction*.

The Grand Human Contradiction

Human beings are unique among animals in the need to balance two opposing drives. The drive to be autonomous—able to decide our own thoughts, imagination, creativity, feelings, and behavior—must compete with an equally strong drive to connect to others. We want to be free and independent without feeling controlled. At the same time, we want to rely on significant others—and have them rely on us—for support and cooperation. Other social animals—those who live in groups and packs and form rudimentary emotional bonds—have relatively little or no discernible sense of individuality to assert and defend. Solitary animals are free and independent but do not form bonds with others that last beyond mother-infancy. Only humans struggle with powerful drives that pull us in opposite directions, where too much emotional investment in one impairs emotional investment in the other.

Competition between the drives for autonomy and connection is so important to human development that it emerges in full force in toddlerhood, which is why the twos can be so terrible. Toddlerhood is the first stage of development in which children seem to realize how separate they are from their caregivers, as they become aware of emotional states that differ from those of their parents. They had previously felt a kind of merging with caregivers, which provided a sense of security and comfort. The new realization of differences stirs excitement and curiosity but also attenuates the comfort and security of the merged state. Now they must struggle with an inchoate sense of self prone to negative identity. They don't know who they are, but when aroused, they know who they're not: they're not whatever you want. Thus we have the favorite two words of the toddler: "Mine!" and "No!"

The increasing conflict with parents wrought by the drive for autonomy presents obstacles to the other powerful human drive: to connect, to value and be valued, to be comforted and to comfort. Hostility toward their parents, however short in duration, stirs uncomfortable feelings of guilt, shame, and anxiety, which fuel intense emotional distress: the classic temper tantrum. Internal emotional conflict is overwhelming for toddlers because they have so little development in the regulatory part of their brains—the PFC.

But for many people, the emotional intensity of those early struggles to balance autonomy with connection forged strong neural pathways in the developing brain. Under stress, these fortified neural patterns—reinforced countless times over the years—hijack higher cognitive processes to validate its alarms and justify its impulsivity and overreactions, instead of modifying them with assessments of reality.

The Two Brains

The downside of late maturity in the Adult brain is that it comes online after the Toddler brain has already formed habits of coping with the alarms it raises, mostly through blame, denial, and avoidance. Many Adult brain interpretations and explanations under stress are dominated by those habits, which lowers the accuracy of its reality-testing and impairs its ability to make viable judgments. To the extent that Toddler brain habits are reinforced in adulthood, the Adult confuses the alarm with reality, which makes Toddler brain alarms self-validating:

"If I'm angry at you, you must be doing something wrong. If I'm anxious, you must be threatening, rejecting, or manipulative."

The result is self-fulfilling prophesy. Other people are bound to react negatively to the negativity I transmit.

Fortunately, the Adult brain has the power to override Toddler brain habits and intentionally develop new ones that serve one's long-term best interests. Developing new habits is not an easy process, but it's utterly necessary to *soaring above*. The first step is to change the way we regard Toddler brain alarms.

Negative Feelings
Are Signals, Not Reality

All alarm systems, negative feelings included, are calibrated to give false positives. You don't want a smoke alarm that doesn't go off until the house is in flames; you want it to go off when there's just a little smoke, even if that means it occasionally gets triggered when someone is cooking or smoking a cigarette. The Toddler brain functions as if the smoke alarm *is* the fire, instead of a signal that a fire might possibly exist. That's like hearing a smoke alarm and screaming, "We're all going to die!" We actually come close to that level of error by assuming that emotional alarms represent certain reality.

The Adult brain reacts to smoke alarms by checking out the signal to see if there really is a fire or just something cooking. If there is a fire, the focus is on putting it out rather than reacting in panic, trying to ignore it, or blaming it on someone. In the Adult brain we pay attention to feelings as important signals but don't validate them as reality. Negative feelings must be regulated with reality checks (is there really a fire?) *and* plans for improvement (Put out the fire).

Reality-testing, appraisal, calculations, judgment, self-regulation, and theory of mind are the tools of the Adult brain. But it is capable of so much more.

The Power to
Create Value and Meaning

Value is a special kind of importance that goes beyond survival and biological needs. To *value* is to make people, things, and ideas important enough to *appreciate, nurture,* and *protect.* We create meaning and purpose in our lives by honoring the value we bestow on people, objects, concepts, behaviors, and some notion of spirituality.

A sunset has value if and only if we give it value—that is, invest energy and effort to fully perceive it, which allows us to appreciate it. While it does nothing for the sunset if we value it, valuing it does wonders for us. The moment of value creation makes us feel more vital, engaged, interested, and appreciative—in short, more *alive.* Life means more at the instant we create value, just as it means less when we're not creating value. Most positive emotion, passion, meaning, purpose, and conviction come from creating and protecting value, and much emptiness, aggression, and depression result from failure to create value.

Humans are unique among animals in our ability to create value and meaning. I call the innate drive to create value (and experience it) *core value.* It includes the instinctual self-worth that makes newborns value and attach to caregivers, with the expectation that the caregivers will meet their emotional needs. Psychologists have known for a long time that babies come out of the womb seeking to be valued. If they are not valued at all, they fail to thrive; they stop metabolizing food and reject medicines on a cellular level. Infants severely deprived of valuing behavior from adults lose the will to live.

A more recent discovery in child development suggests that being valued is not enough. Infants also need their own expressions of value to be accepted by their caregivers. For example, the majority of mothers with debilitating depression are able to love their children and care for them. But many also feel uncomfortable receiving love from them. Infants express love by mirroring caregiver smiles, reaching out, cooing, and widening their eyes for more connection through eye contact. Some depressed mothers feel a need to turn away from these behaviors but not in deliberate attempts to reject their babies. A more subtle discomfort outside their awareness causes them to turn away from the children they love.

To understand the experience of these depressed women, think of times when you've felt down, blue, or even slightly depressed. At those times it was a little uncomfortable to hold eye contact in social contexts, even intimate ones. It was a bit harder than normal to receive compliments, praise, or affection because, in some vague way, it seemed like you were getting something you didn't deserve and something you couldn't quite gather the energy to return. Oh, you knew intellectually that you deserved it, but the subtle, unconscious sense of unworthiness remained. That same sense of unworthiness, experienced as a vague discomfort, makes some depressed caregivers turn away from babies who try to express love. As a result, their infants, though cared for, also become depressed.

Virtually all our accomplishments in life occur through Adult brain value-creation, and all our failures owe to devaluing (value-destruction), which typically occurs in the Toddler brain. Consider who is more likely to maintain healthy weight: the person who values health, or the one who devalues her body? Who is more likely to succeed with fewer mistakes: the coach who values the skills and cohesiveness of the team, or the one who devalues his players? Who will do better at work and feel more satisfied with it: the employee who values her contribution and coworkers, or the one who devalues his job, peers, or managers? Who is more likely to thrive after intimate betrayal: the betrayed partner who values her well-being, her other relationships, her strengths and resilience, or the one who devalues his life and most of the people in it?

High value investment increases meaning, purpose, and vitality, with stronger motivations to create, build, improve, appreciate, connect, and protect. Value investment literally boosts the immune system and makes us physically healthier. As value investment declines, so do vitality, motivation, meaning, purpose, and health. You begin to function more on automatic pilot with less interest and positive energy. If value investment declines too far, you begin to feel numb or depressed. If it declines drastically, you lose the will to live.

Anthropologists report that the earliest humans decorated rocks to make them special. More important, they made themselves special by creating and appreciating the decorated rocks. We become more valuable as we create and appreciate value, and we become less valuable (able to value) as we devalue our surroundings and the people in them.

While value investment provides a greater sense of being alive, value destruction diminishes the will to live. In the long run, if you devalue more than you value, your life will be pretty bad, even if a lot of good things happen to you. I've had considerable evidence of this, since my frequent media appearances have attracted some rich, famous, and powerful clients whose lives are filled with good fortune. Yet it's amazing how creative they are at finding ways to make themselves miserable, simply because they choose to devalue more than they value.

On the other side of the coin, if you value more than you devalue, your life will be good, even if a lot of bad things happen. My primary example is a mother I knew who had lost both her teenage sons. Within a year of each other, one son died in an accident, and the other was killed while defending a preteen girl, whom he didn't know, from a bully's unwanted advances. Out of nowhere, this woman's only children were taken from her. Yet she turned the deaths of her sons into inspiration for other members of the community through her impassioned advocacy for various youth groups. She was the most charismatic and genuine person I've ever met because, despite the enormity of her misfortunes, she valued more than she devalued.

Value vs. Preferences and Pleasure

It's possible to live without much value in your life. But such a life, as Hamlet would put it, would be "dull, flat, and unprofitable." Acting consistently on the uniquely human drive to create and protect value provides a sense of meaning and purpose to life that endures well beyond the momentary satisfactions of pleasure, enjoyment, or meeting one's preferences. For example, I love ice cream, but it provides no meaning or purpose to my life. I love my family, who collectively and individually provide enormous meaning and purpose to my life. Although I love the momentary pleasure of ice cream, I never feel guilty or ashamed when I don't eat it. (In fact, eating too much causes guilt and shame, as overindulging any preference violates a deeper value of health and well-being.) But I certainly feel guilty and ashamed when I fail to nurture, appreciate, and protect my family. Guilt and shame keep us true to our deeper values. Yet we subvert this vital function with the toddler coping mechanisms of blame, denial, and avoidance, and this subversion undermines the ability to create value and meaning in life and makes us more likely to confuse preferences with value.

Toddlers experience pleasure, and they certainly have strong preferences. But creating value, beyond rudimentary emotional bonds, is something we need to do in the Adult brain.

Psychotherapy of Value

It was clear as we neared the end of our first therapy session that Tom had worked hard to cultivate an ironic sense of humor. So I expected some witty remark to try to lighten the tone as he looked down at his fingers, toying with the loose fabric of the chair in my office. Still, I was in no way prepared for what he said on that summer afternoon some twenty years ago.

"I guess I'm just another middle-aged guy looking for a rainbow," he sighed.

Maybe it was the shadowy tone of voice or the thinness of his smile immediately after he said it. For whatever reason, Tom's little statement completely disarmed my empirically based symptom-reduction training that had already yielded a treatment strategy. Suddenly I realized that the ebb and flow of his emotions were not merely symptoms crying out for therapy—specifically, teaching him how to use the power of the Adult brain to outgrow the hurt and how to change the coping habits of the Toddler brain. Knowing that you can't enjoy a country drive if the spark plugs in your car are misfiring gives you no idea of what it takes to appreciate the beautiful scenery all along the drive. Tom did not simply need help with his spark plugs.

My practice, while highly successful in reducing symptoms at one-year follow-up, was, before Tom, about spark plugs, having to do with emotion regulation skills—making the emotional system stronger and more flexible. This is important, to be sure. But a more profound kind of importance is about value. We experience value as *self-enhancement*, becoming better through the appreciation of someone or something and through investment of time, energy, effort, and sacrifice—above and beyond spark-plug considerations. Doodling is spark plug (nervous discharge); drawing is value. Using the stars as a compass or calendar is spark plug; appreciating their beauty is value. Having sex is of spark-plug importance; making love is about value. Influencing the behavior of loved ones is spark plug; compassion for them is value.

It became clear to me on that afternoon with Tom that the services I offered had to help people create and invest more value in their lives, that is, to get the fullest benefits of the Adult brain. I had to do more than help Tom weather the storm; I had to show him how to appreciate whatever rainbow he found, and, in a real sense, to become the rainbow. As T. S. Eliot would have it, you become the music while the music lasts. In marriage, for instance, if you do not become the love, the love will not last.

The rest of this book is committed to using the full power of your Adult brain to create value, meaning, and purpose.

CHAPTER 2

How We Make
the Same Mistakes
Over and Over

If you sometimes feel like you make the same mistakes over and over, you're definitely not alone. Everyone on Earth is capable of repeating the same mistakes again and again. Everyone can react to a jerk like a jerk. We can all fall into relationships filled with cold shoulders, boredom, or high conflict. And we're all sadly capable of turning pain into suffering.

We repeatedly shoot ourselves in the foot for one simple reason. Under stress, we tend to retreat to habits of emotion regulation formed as far back as toddlerhood. Our thought processes become self-obsessed, and our feelings veer toward the volatile, if not a full-blown roller-coaster. We're likely to act impulsively, with little

17

foresight. The only available solutions seem like "No!" and "Mine!" ("My way!")

Why We Repeat Mistakes

The Toddler brain is dominated by feelings rather than analysis of facts. (If the feelings are negative, they seem like alarms.) Not surprising, habits formed in the Toddler brain are activated by feelings rather than analysis of the conditional context of past mistakes and their consequences. When we feel that way again, for any reason, past behavioral impulses grow stronger, increasing the likelihood of repeating the mistake. We're likely to eat the whole cake and then realize that we should have had a V8 instead. We'll throw a temper tantrum (or repress one) before remembering the resolution to take a time-out. We'll pout, criticize, or devalue others instead of seeking to improve and repair. The dominance of feelings—over judgment, analysis, foresight, and sensitivity to other perspectives—is why diets don't work, addicts relapse, projects fail, marriages falter, and Mr. Hyde can't remember what Dr. Jekyll learned in anger management class.

Virtually all the people I've had the honor to treat in more than thirty years of clinical practice have presented with entrenched habits of retreating to the Toddler brain when things get tough. Unlike personality, genetics, and temperament, habits are readily changeable, although the change process is often tedious and repetitious. I cannot emphasize strongly enough that once habits are formed, they are not changed by insight or understanding of how they started. They can be changed only by establishing new habits.

The Toddler Brain Is Self-Obsessed, Volatile, All-or-Nothing

Toddlers are incapable of seeing any perspective other than their own. (Perspective-taking—understanding how other people experience the world—is a higher-order operation of the Adult brain.) Toddlers use imagination to fill in the huge gaps in their knowledge of other people's perspectives. But their imaginations are dominated by how they feel at the moment, and how they feel at this moment is unlikely to be how they felt a few moments ago, as feelings in the Toddler brain are highly volatile. Their attributions about other people tend to vacillate between the very positive and very negative. This subjects them to what psychologists call "splitting," the wellspring of adult "all-or-nothing" thinking. You're either all good or all bad; they love you or hate you; they think the best or the worst about you. You probably know adults who put you on a pedestal when they feel good and cast you as a demon when they feel bad. They become needy or aloof. They cling or pout. If their feelings are hostile, they're prone to passive aggression and even violence.

It doesn't take much experience with a toddler to recognize periods of neediness and bouts of pouting. Less obvious is passive-aggressive behavior, which is a toddler way of asserting autonomy. Video studies of toddlers show them doing things like intentionally dropping objects as a way of saying "No," purposely making noise when their parents are on the phone, telling fibs about other kids, using one parent against the other, and faking injuries—or actually hurting themselves—to get rewarded or avoid a reprimand. Adults in their Toddler brains try to feel more autonomous by moralizing, preaching, lecturing, psychoanalyzing, acting like martyrs, or devaluing and demeaning others. And then there's violence.

Take the following violence-prone quiz, in which you identify the family member to whom the question or statement most likely refers.

1. Who are the most violent people in the vast majority of families? _____

2. This family member often uses anger as a defense. _____

3. If this family member doesn't get his/her way, violence is likely. _____

4. If hurt or offended, this family member wants to hit or throw something. _____

Did you guess that the correct answer for each question is not "father" or "mother," but a child under three? The trick of the quiz is in the word "violence," which makes us think of damage. Most toddlers do little or no damage with their violence—they'll hit you with a tissue or stomp their feet, scream, or flail at the air—so we tend not to think of their behavior as violent, although it is. The point is that aggressive anger and violence (when not protecting life, limb, or other people) is not adult; it's childish. It comes from the Toddler brain and needs regulation by the Adult brain.

How Can I Be Me When They're Being Them?

Emotional reactivity is an automatic response to specific events, situations, or people. Sometimes this is a great thing. While falling in love, the mere presence of the beloved fills us with fascination and joy. We thrill at the smiles of our infants and revel in the excitement of new friends. But under stress, emotional reactivity is almost entirely negative. The environment seems more threatening or fraught with uncertainty. Our buttons get pushed more easily. We're more likely to lash out or, if we hold it in, emotionally shut down. In families afflicted with high emotional reactivity, a negative feeling in one causes chaos or withdrawal in the others.

All animals are subject to high emotional reactivity when the environment is perceived as dangerous. The hair-trigger response that shoots adrenaline and cortisol into their bloodstreams keeps them ever prepared for flight or fight. The problem with fight-or-flight reactions for modern humans living in much safer environments than our ancestors is that the brain is a better-safe-than-sorry system. It would rather be wrong 999 times thinking your spouse is a saber-toothed tiger than be wrong once thinking a saber-toothed tiger is your spouse.

Toddler Brain Reactaholism

Just about anyone or anything can stimulate painful emotional reactions when stress triggers a habit of retreating to the Toddler brain—the alarm-driven limbic system. Then the only certainty we can have is saying, "No!" or "Mine!" In the worst case, we can turn into reactaholics, feeling that we have to react negatively to others to maintain a sense of self. Toddler brain reactaholism is the number-one addiction of our times. The other addictions tend to start as attempts to ease the chronic powerlessness and frequent ill feelings of reactaholism.

The aspect of emotional reactivity that makes it difficult to see, let alone change, is its illusion of free will. We think that we're acting of our own volition when we're merely reacting to someone else's negativity. We've all uttered, or at least thought, the most ironic of all statements, "You're not going to bring me down!" As long as we're in the Toddler brain, we're already down, reacting to negativity with negativity.

To lower their anxiety about getting their buttons pushed, Toddler brain reactaholics try hard to control the behavior of others. My client Celine, like the vast majority of controlling people I have known, constantly told her beleaguered husband what to do and when and where to do it. From her perspective, she had to, because it felt as if *his* behavior entirely controlled her emotions. If he left the towel on the bathroom floor, she felt overwhelmed with resentment and anger. "I get tense walking down the hall, because I know when I get to the bathroom, I'll see that he's left the toilet seat up again," she told me. Of course, Celine's attempts to control her husband made him *less* cooperative. In case you haven't noticed, human beings hate to feel controlled and will rarely cooperate when they do. The couple regularly got into Toddler brain standoffs of "Mine!" and "No!"

In the Toddler brain, thinking about the future is nearly impossible. When Celine considered making plans, she inevitably imagined her husband refusing to cooperate and could feel the anger surging through her body in response. To avoid such unpleasant thoughts, she stopped thinking about the future altogether. This habitual avoidance of goal setting is one reason that Toddler brain reactaholics never achieve their full potential in life. Instead of setting goals and planning how to reach them, they try to avoid certain kinds of situations and people. Because so many people and situations have the power to push their buttons, Toddler brain reactaholics never know how they'll feel from one moment to the next. They can scarcely develop a consistent sense of self because they're different with each person who "makes" them react differently. If I'm one person with you and another with him and yet another with her, pretty soon I won't know who the hell I am. The Toddler brain's struggle for autonomy rages on, at the cost of connections to others and with the failure to feel authentic. Toddler brain reactaholism makes it seem that your feelings are not about you; they're about whoever is causing the reaction at the moment. This alienation from internal experience undermines a sense of autonomy and exacerbates the feelings of powerlessness inherent in reactaholism.

A quick way to tell if you're a reactaholic is to notice how you approach a workplace meeting. You may well be a reactaholic if you don't know what you will do until someone else gives you something to which you can react in a definite (usually ego-defensive) way. I once witnessed just such a circumstance while giving a lecture to a group of managers about resentment in the workplace. Many of the participants were not sure why the presentation was on the agenda. While most were open to whatever new ideas might be put forth, a couple of reactaholics were in the room. When introducing me, the company's owner joked about having never heard of resentment in the workplace.

"We don't have resentment in my division," one of the supervisors said dismissively after the owner's comment. I had been observing the body language and facial expressions of the participants during the opening remarks. This guy was one of the two who had no opinion about the topic, until he misconstrued his boss's joke to be a criticism of the HR manager who had engaged me. Then he became convinced that my presentation would be a waste of time. Reacting to him, the other participant whose body language was indecisive about the presentation became just as convinced that his colleague was wrong.

"You sound awfully resentful in saying that," he said to his colleague, only half-joking. "You're living proof that we need this material."

The next time you go into any kind of meeting, at work or in the community, note how you feel about the issues on the agenda and then see if they change or become more intense in reaction to someone at the meeting.

Here's another little test of reactaholism:

1. Are you concerned about getting your buttons pushed?

2. Do you ever worry about how you're going to react at work or at home? _____

3. Do you brace yourself before you walk in to the house? When you're home, do you tense up when you hear your partner close the front door? _____

4. Do you tense up when you get near certain people at work?

   _____

5. Do you not bring up certain things because you don't want to think about the response you might get? _____

6. Do you find it hard to think about the future? _____

The only way to triumph over Toddler brain reactivity is to hold on to your self-value under stress so you don't feel devalued by the behavior or attitudes of other people. That requires switching into the Adult brain when you most need it. It's a skill anyone can learn and everyone must master to have any chance at a consistently happy life. The goal of this book is to help you develop that skill. The alternative turns the pain of life into suffering, which is the topic of the next chapter.

CHAPTER 3

How Pain Becomes Suffering

When toddlers feel something, they can't imagine ever not having felt that way or that they will ever feel differently in the future. Their feelings seem permanent and unchangeable. To be fair, memory of past emotional states is brief even for adults. Psychologists call the phenomenon *state-dependent recall*; information learned in one mood or emotional state is most likely to be recalled in a similar mood or emotional state. When resentful toward a spouse, you can remember everything he/she did to offend or disappoint since the day you married. But you'll recall only nice things about your spouse when you feel sweet and loving. When depressed, we tend to think of only sad things, and when we're happy, we tend to think exclusively of happy events. When we're angry, we think of offensive things, and when compassionate, we recall our more humane experiences. When feeling helpless and dependent, we forget that we're fairly competent and creative most of the time.

Negative emotional states are especially susceptible to state-dependent recall, due to their more urgent survival importance. If a saber-toothed tiger swatted at early humans from the side, that information was necessary for survival. However, it wasn't necessary to have it in consciousness all the time, where the intensity of the memory would impair performance of other important tasks that require conscious attention. So the information is "filed" under fight-or-flight arousal and recalled only during similar arousal. (The flashbacks of PTSD constitute a *breakdown* of state-dependent recall, which allows memories of extreme threat to intrude on relatively benign emotional states.)

State-dependent recall is generally an efficient mode of information processing. But the emotional state that leads to most self-defeating behavior—anger—is processed in milliseconds (thousandths of a second) and cannot be selective in recall. We tend to feel the urgency of attack every time something happens to stimulate anger. This response is helpful if the stimulus is really a saber-toothed tiger, but not so great if the challenge is a stubborn teenager, distracted spouse, rude driver, or narcissistic coworker.

State-dependent recall keeps us in whatever part of the brain we're in at the moment, simply because we're accessing only those memories associated with the current emotional state. When feeling helpless in the Toddler brain, it seems that we've always been helpless. When feeling dependent, it seems that we were always dependent on someone else or some substance. When depressed, it seems that we never felt well. When feeling destructive, it seems that we've always been devalued, disrespected, disregarded, angry, or bitter.

Fortunately, state-dependent recall works in the Adult brain, too. When feeling compassionate, we can't remember ever feeling resentful. And when feeling confident, we're apt to forget mistakes we've made in the past, while implicitly remembering the corrections we made. For example, I won't remember in the Adult brain banging my thumb with a hammer, but I'll implicitly recall how to hold the nail and swing the hammer for maximum efficiency.

Despite the illusions of state-dependent recall, negative feelings are transitory. A toddler can express hatred for you in a temper tantrum and a few minutes later climb onto your lap in loving affection.

The negative feelings that lead to repeating mistakes over and over last a long time *only* when we try to justify violations of our deeper values. For instance, the subtle guilt I'd feel for being attracted to a movie actress would last much longer if I were to justify the attraction by thinking of times my wife disappointed me (ignoring the times I disappointed her). Justifying emotions amplifies, magnifies, and prolongs them. In the Adult brain, we know that negative emotions are either motivations (my subtle guilt goes away once I follow its motivation to connect with my wife), or, if it's a bad mood, it will pass, like the flu or a cold. In the Toddler brain, negative feelings seem eternal.

Mistakes we repeat with regularity rise from the Toddler brain. They turn short-term setbacks into long-term losses and temporary pain into long-term suffering. In the Adult brain, we learn from past mistakes, grow from them, and soar above them.

Emotions vs. Feelings

Emotions *move* us. The word *emotion*, derived from the Latin, literally means "to move." The ancients believed that emotions move behavior; in modern times we say they motivate behavior. They prepare us to do things by sending powerful chemical signals to the muscles and organs of the body.

Feelings are the conscious and most misunderstood component of emotions. In contrast to the simplicity of basic behavioral motivations—approach, avoid, attack—feelings are complex, ever-changing, and subject to moods (like depression), sensations (like warmth, cold, pleasure, pain, comfort, discomfort), and physiological states (like metabolism, hormonal variations, hunger, thirst, and tiredness). All these can seem like "feelings," and that is why people often give psychological meaning to anything that feels uncomfortable. Discomfort seems close enough to negative emotions to keep us hopelessly confused, as long as we're in the Toddler brain, where the focus is on feelings rather than effective behavior. When a toddler is uncomfortable, you had better look out! Same with adults stuck in the Toddler brain.

As part of the human motivational system, feelings are not ends in themselves but a means of getting our attention, so we'll act on

the motivation of the present emotion. For instance, if you're interested in something and don't focus on it, the usually unconscious
emotion of interest starts to feel like anticipation, excitement, a
nagging hunch, or anxiety. If you have ignored someone you love
and don't approach to kiss and make up, the usually unconscious
emotion of guilt will begin to feel like impatience, frustration, anxiety, or depression. If you're in the Toddler brain, you're likely to
blame it on your partner. If you do, the unconscious guilt becomes
anger and resentment, as in, "She had it coming!" or "Why should
I feel sorry for him?"

When we act on the basic motivation of emotions, we're usually
aware of few or no feelings. That's how you can get interested in
something, look up at the clock, and notice that several hours have
passed during which you were largely unaware of any feelings. It's
also how you can pay no attention to someone you love and be
sincerely surprised or defensive when he accuses you of ignoring
him, which you were entirely unaware of doing when interested in
something else. Of course, you can become aware of feelings if you
reflect on them, but that will often stop the motivation and change
the behavior, as well as distort the feeling. For instance, you can
probably recall a romantic moment, like walking on the beach or
lying in front of a cozy fireplace, when your partner almost ruined
it by asking, "What are you feeling right now?" You had to stop
sharing interest, enjoyment, and intimacy to think about what it
feels like to share interest, enjoyment, and intimacy.

The Toddler brain is dominated by feelings, with no awareness of the motivational function of emotions. Feelings become

an end in themselves rather than part of a motivational system. The problem for adults who get stuck in the Toddler brain is that thousands of experiences over a lifetime have conditioned a rather limited number of feelings. For instance, you may have associated feeling shame with your mother's raised eyebrow, your father closing the door to his study, a teacher who made you feel dumb, the text your boyfriend read while you talked to him, as well as many other experiences. Any of these—or anything remotely like them—can trigger confusing "feelings," when motivation is weak and we're more prone to Toddler brain regression. For example, if you are not really interested in learning facts related to a task at work, the look on your boss's face might drop you into the Toddler brain by reminding you of your mother's disdain whenever you disappointed her as a child. This association made during low-interest motivation will feel enough like shame to disorganize your thought processes, inhibit your ability to remember relevant facts, and probably result in mistakes. However, if the motivation to learn is strong—that is, you're really interested in the task—your boss's facial expression will make no difference—you'll remain task-oriented in the Adult brain. Similarly, if the motivation to connect with the texting boyfriend is weak, the Toddler brain response of jealousy will prevail, making you feel less loving and attractive. But if the desire to connect is strong, the Adult brain will regard the texting as a minor bump in the road and try more loving ways of connecting, which are more likely to succeed.

The Psychology of Emotional "Need"

The dominance of feelings in the Toddler brain leads a person to confuse *preferences*—what they would like to have—with *needs*—what they must have. In the Toddler brain, all strong feelings represent emotional "needs." Adults who get stuck in the Toddler brain under stress create hell, or at least purgatory, when they perceive themselves to have emotional needs.

An *emotional need* is a preference you've decided must be gratified to maintain equilibrium: you can't be well or feel whole without it. The perception of need begins with a rise in emotional intensity, feeling more strongly about being with someone or having something. As the intensity increases, it can feel like you "need" to do or have it for one compelling reason: It's the *same emotional process as biological need*. (You can observe the biological process by planting your face in a pillow; emotional intensity rises just before you struggle to breathe. Or think of how emotional intensity increases when your get near home after a long drive, just *before* the urge to urinate grows acute.) When emotion suddenly rises, as it does when reminded of the girlfriend who dumped you, your brain confuses preferences with biological needs. In other words, the perception of need becomes self-reinforcing: "I feel it, therefore, I need it, and if I need it, I have to feel it more."

In terms of motivation, perceived emotional needs are similar to addictions, without the intense stimulation of reward centers in the brain when gratified or the cellular contraction in various parts of the body during withdrawal. You might say that the body decides that you have an addiction, while the conscious brain decides that you have a need. But once the brain decides that it needs something, pursuit of it can be just as compelling as addiction.

It's easy to confuse wanting with needing in a culture that readily conflates the two. "Getting your needs met" has become the motto of the times. We "look out for number one" by construing preferences as needs and striving at all costs to get them met. My preferences are superior to yours because mine are "needs," while yours are just ego fluff. Some authors suggest that you can't feel secure at work merely by doing an outstanding job; you must make yourself "needed," not by your hard work, but through manipulation. Desire is not enough for Toddler brain love. "I need you" feels better than "I want you."

Adults have only one emotional "need," and that is to act consistently on deeper values. If we do that, all the preferences that seem like emotional needs will either be satisfied as a byproduct of meaningful living, or they'll be deemed unimportant in the course of a purposeful life. The best chance of attaining the life you most want to have is to approach it out of *desire*—that is, from the Adult brain—not from the *emotional neediness* of the Toddler brain.

Where Pain Becomes Suffering

As a lifesaving alarm system, pain keeps us focused on distress for the purpose of relieving it. Pain motivates behavior that will help heal, repair, or improve. A pain in the foot, for example, motivates taking the rock off it, getting more comfortable shoes, soaking it in a tub of warm water, or visiting a podiatrist.

If we do not act on the motivation to heal-repair-improve, or fail in our attempts to do so, the alarm of pain intensifies and generalizes. The toothache becomes facial pain; the sore foot seems to throb along the whole side of the body. When pain intensifies and generalizes over time, it becomes suffering. Suffering is repeated failure to act successfully on the natural motivation of pain to do something that will heal, repair, or improve. In the Toddler brain, we're more likely to focus on the alarm and ignore the motivation to heal, repair, or improve. In the Toddler brain, pain becomes suffering.

Like its physical counterpart, normal psychological pain (not caused by brain disease or severe disorder) is localized in the beginning, usually in the form of guilt or anxiety about something specific. Also like physical pain, failure to act on the motivation to heal-repair-improve intensifies and generalizes the alarm. Guilt becomes shame (feeling inadequate or defective) or depression (nothing matters), and anxiety becomes chronic dread or inability to relax, sleeplessness, and hypervigilance—expecting danger everywhere.

When it comes to emotional pain, the behavior choices that will heal, repair, or improve are not always clear. As psychological pain generalizes, it seems to be about the self—a kind of self-ache. (In the Toddler brain, everything is about the newly emerging sense of self.) As the alarm of pain intensifies, it strengthens focus on our own distress, making us self-obsessed. Eventually we identify with the pain, in a subtle or overt victim identity. At that point, we can scarcely perceive other people's pain that does not seem to match our own experience. This heightened self-obsession makes the alarm of pain louder and more general, impeding genuine connections that heal and promote growth.

Those who suffer psychologically have gotten into the habit of trying to numb or avoid the pain signals that would otherwise motivate healing, repairing, or improving. They inadvertently turn pain into suffering by virtue of *toddler coping mechanisms*, which we take up in the next chapter.

CHAPTER 4

Feeling Powerful vs. Being Powerful

"Coping" in the Toddler Brain

Coping mechanisms are adaptations to environmental stress designed to comfort or give a sense of control. They differ from the old notion of unconscious defense mechanisms, which Freud believed defended the ego from unacceptable impulses, such as sexual feelings for or hostility toward parents or caregivers. Coping mechanisms are generally conscious, intentional, and often tactical or strategic.

Toddlers use coping mechanisms primarily to ward off threats to autonomy and connection, because they cannot keep these competing drives in balance. For example, if you go into a room to find a toddler alone with a broken lamp and ask what happened, you'll hear, "Someone else did it" (blame) or "I don't know" (denial), or the kid hides or runs away (avoidance). Psychologists used to believe that toddlers used blame, denial, and avoidance merely as attempts to avoid punishment and indirectly assert autonomy. Now we understand that they're also trying to maintain or reinstate connection. After all, the real pain of punishment isn't the sanction administered: a time-out or spanking. The grave pain of punishment is the Toddler brain's experience of rejection and loss of connection.

Whatever short-term gain there might be for adults when we blame, deny responsibility, or avoid, emotional experience and social reprimand will most certainly come back to haunt us, sooner rather than later, usually in the form of resentful coworkers and family members.

Denial and avoidance are fairly universal and straightforward. (If you're married, you're probably convinced your spouse uses them all the time.) *Denial* can seem like stubbornness, deception, and insensitivity. It's sometimes those things, too, but it's also an attempt to assert autonomy at the cost of connection ("Just suck it up like I do!") or gain connection at the cost of personal integrity ("I didn't flirt. I love you!"). Adults in the Toddler brain tend to favor indirect *avoidance* tactics, including procrastination, stonewalling, overworking, overdrinking, overeating, over exercising, and so on. The most direct and usually the most damaging of the toddler coping mechanisms is *blame*.

The Road to Psychological
Ruin Begins with Blame

If you feel bad about anything at all and blame it on someone else, what can you then do to make yourself feel better?

Not a thing. The act of blame renders you powerless, which is the internal source of all the frustration, anger, and resentment that go with blame. More important, blame strips painful emotions of their primary function, which is to motivate corrective behavior. As we saw in the previous chapter, pain—physical and psychological—is part of an alarm network that evolved to keep you safe and well. The function of guilt, shame, and anxiety is not to punish you. Their primary function is to motivate behavior that heals, corrects, or improves.

For example, guilt is about violating your values; the motivation of guilt is to act according to your values. Acting according to your deeper values is the only thing that resolves guilt. Shame is about failure and inadequacy; the motivation is to reevaluate, reconceptualize, and redouble efforts to achieve success, or if the failure is in attachment, to be more loving or compassionate. Those are the only things that will resolve shame. Anxiety is a dread of something bad occurring that will exceed or deplete resources; the motivation is to learn more about what might happen and develop plans to cope with it. Blame, denial, and avoidance might give momentary relief of guilt, shame, and anxiety but will soon worsen them by blocking their natural motivations.

Even a destructive emotion like jealousy has a motivation to heal, improve, and repair. A toddler who sees his parents hugging and kissing is likely to feel a stab of jealousy, which makes him feel left out and abandoned, and that makes him feel unlovable. His first instinct is to wedge himself between his mother and father and be as cute and loving as he possibly can be, to reattach and strengthen their bond. If his parents respond to his loving efforts with acceptance and affection, his feelings of being loved and lovable are reinforced. He will grow more secure in his basic worthiness of love, which allows him to become more tolerant of his parents' expressions of affection for each other. But if his embracing parents grow annoyed with his "intrusion" or regard him as "spoiled," they might push him away or chastise him as "selfish." In that case he learns to interpret his pain as a sign of failure, inadequacy, and unworthiness. Stripped of the natural way to relieve his vulnerability, he feels powerless. Instead of becoming more loving when he feels bad, he becomes angry or resentful (blame), pretends it doesn't matter (denial), or tries to focus on something else (avoidance).

We'll return to jealousy later. The point here is to emphasize that emotions are part of a motivational system; they exist not to punish but to motivate behavior that will help. Negative emotions do not indicate that you're bad; they tell you to do better. They're correction messages, not failure messages.

If you feel that your emotions are punishment, you will feel unfairly treated by other people, particularly loved ones. You'll blame the very guilt, shame, and anxiety that evolved to make you more loving toward them. Once blame becomes a habit, it poisons your relationships and your very sense of self. It keeps you locked in the Toddler brain—a high price to pay for the temporary advantage of transferring guilt and shame onto others.

Blame vs. Solving Problems

Blame makes it almost impossible to find solutions to problems. Besides locking us in the Toddler brain, blame puts us in the wrong dimension of time. It's always about the past—specifically, who caused the bad thing to happen. When I speak to groups, I usually ask for a show of hands to indicate how many people are able to go back to the past to solve a problem. Solutions, of course, must occur in the present and future.

Blame further obscures solutions by locking us into the problem. We focus on how bad it is and whose fault it is rather than on ways to improve. To justify blame, we focus on the damage or injury we've suffered, when growth and well-being require resilience, intelligence, and creativity.

Blame tends to make bad situations worse by putting us in punishment mode, rather than in improvement mode. In punishment mode, we're likely to make everyone around us defensive and resistant. Even if we get people to do what we want, they'll do it grudgingly, with hidden and often not-so-hidden resentment.

The bottom line is that we must choose between blaming and solving problems, because we cannot do both at the same time. Blame is a Toddler brain coping mechanism; solving problems is the domain of the Adult brain.

Blame and the
Natural Purpose of Anger

Blame perverts the primary function of anger, which, in humans, is not self-protection. (If you doubt that, consider when you're likely to get angrier: when I attack you, or your children.) The survival purpose of anger is to protect loved ones, which overrides self-protection. Most people who witnessed their children being harmed would experience enough rage to take on an assailant many times larger and stronger. The reason that humans are the only mammals that consistently use aggression against attachment figures is that we've developed a specialized, defensive form of anger unique among Earth's inhabitants. It's called *resentment*. While the primary purpose of anger is protection of loved ones, the purpose of resentment is protection of the ego. And no one can hurt our egos as much as loved ones.

Because their egos are newly emergent, toddlers resent a lot, although they don't hold on to it for very long. Adults in the Toddler brain can hold on to resentment forever, thanks to their need to justify any negative emotion that might violate deeper values. The more we justify resentment, the stronger it feels, and the stronger it feels, the more we have to justify it. Resentment serves the ego in the short run by transferring guilt and shame through blame, but weakens the ego in the long run with chronic feelings of powerlessness. The more fragile the ego, the more we blame. The more we blame, the more fragile the ego becomes, and the more likely we are to subvert the natural function of anger by turning against loved ones.

How to Be *Wrong*
Even When You're *Right*

Blame-driven resentment makes you wrong, even if you're right. You can start out factually correct, but if you fail to appreciate other people's perspectives, you'll soon get resentful and probably angry, and so will everyone around you. Resentment and anger *simplify*, *amplify*, and *magnify* negative stimuli. They make you reduce the object of your resentment or anger to one or two negative aspects. That's fine if you're dealing with a saber-toothed tiger, because then you don't need to know about its kittenhood or the number of cubs it has to feed back at the den or whether it's on the endangered species list. You reduce it to one negative aspect—the threat it poses—and you either attack or retreat.

But in human relationships, amplification, magnification, and oversimplification *distort* issues by blowing them out of proportion and taking them out of context. It's easier to see how this works when you are the recipient of someone's resentment or anger. Think of a time when people were resentful or angry at you, and they were factually right: you *did* make a mistake or do something wrong. Even though they were right, you probably felt they were making too much of it or overlooking crucial details or *reducing* you to that one mistake, as if all the good things you've ever done in your life didn't count. Well, other people react to your resentment and anger in the same way. Most humans subjected to the amplification, magnification, and oversimplification of resentment or anger get resentful, contentious, or sulky in return, just like you do.

Resentment also creates hyperfocus on one's own perspective to the *exclusion* of everyone else's. Did you ever go out to lunch with someone resentful about something that happened that morning at work and try to talk about anything other than what he's upset about? You could probably say, "I was thinking about killing myself last night," and you'd get a reply of, "Oh, really? But did you hear what she said to me this morning?" Of course this hyperfocus makes it impossible to see another person's perspective, which creates a prison of self-obsession in the Toddler brain.

Resentment *wounds* relationships at work, but it *kills* close relationships. Blame-driven resentment and the anger that rises from it are for dominating and devaluing, not for negotiating or improving relationships. If you're resentful or angry when discussing family finances, for instance, you don't just want your spouse to agree with you, you want her to feel stupid for not agreeing with you. Resentment and anger exist exclusively to devalue, reject, warn, threaten, intimidate, or attack—in your head or in reality, behind their backs or in their faces. You may feel as if you're doing these things defensively, but you are nevertheless rejecting, warning, threatening, intimidating, or attacking.

You can trust that resentment in the workplace will increase complaints, absenteeism, turnover, tardiness, healthcare utilization, and sabotage. At home it causes disconnection, alienation, abuse, and divorce.

Feeling Powerful vs. Being Powerful

The new mobility that toddlers experience makes them feel more powerful. At the same time, their utter dependency on their caregivers makes them feel powerless, which threatens their emerging sense of autonomy. So it's perfectly understandable that toddlers use coping mechanisms to feel more powerful momentarily, even though blame, denial, and avoidance actually make them less powerful. It's not so understandable when adults, with their powerful prefrontal cortex, repeatedly do the same.

I grew up with angry and resentful people and have struggled my whole career to help thousands of resentful and angry clients achieve a better life. The hardest truth for any of them to grasp is the difference between feeling powerful and being powerful. Most anger and resentment are attempts to feel powerful at the cost of being powerful.

Anger is activated in all mammals by a dual perception of vulnerability and threat, which is why wounded animals are so ferocious. In humans, most anger results from blaming the feelings of vulnerability—guilt, shame, anxiety—on someone else, whom we then perceive as a threat. The feeling of power gained from anger is transitory, coming from the amphetamine effect of the adrenaline spurt that fuels it. Amphetamine effects create a sense of power and confidence; it feels like you can do anything! Like all amphetamine effects, the sense of power and confidence gained from anger resolves in depleted energy, self-doubt, and a diminished sense of self. It always drops you down lower than where you started, which is why most people feel depressed after a bout of anger.

In the Toddler brain, we try to cut off those hills and valleys with persistent resentment. As a low-grade, defensive form of anger, resentment lacks sufficient adrenaline to cause the immediate overreactions of its more intense cousin, but it has enough of the effect to ward off self-doubt and maintain the feeling of being right. This mediating effect of resentment makes it self-reinforcing in that it creates the need it temporarily gratifies. That is, the blame inherent in resentment makes us powerless, while its adrenaline makes us temporarily feel more powerful. Like resentment, drugs make you feel better for a while then much worse, creating a need to feel better again by taking the drug. People justifying resentment sound like alcoholics describing the "trace" vitamins in beer, which makes consumption of large quantities a health necessity.

We'll see in later chapters how to *be* powerful and eliminate the doomed Toddler brain quest to *feel* powerful. Hopefully by now it's apparent that the toddler coping mechanisms of blame, denial, and avoidance make us feel powerful for a time but render us powerless over our thoughts, feelings, and behavior. If you wouldn't drive a car designed by a toddler, don't use coping mechanisms designed by a toddler.

Next we'll see how toddler coping mechanisms form entrenched habits that ruin the very best of adult intentions.

CHAPTER 5

Toddler Brain Habits Ruin the Best of Intentions

T he autonomy struggle of toddlers is evident during a brief developmental stage when they impulsively hit, kick, scratch, bite, pull hair, or otherwise act aggressively. For most children, this behavioral tendency is short-lived, devoid of ill will or cruelty. Although troubling to many parents, this aggressive stage is normal and, managed properly, passes without harm.

The explanation for toddler aggression when I was in doctoral training was that humans are basically uncivilized, so toddlers must be trained in social rules to curtail aggressive impulses. Thankfully, better research since then offers a more informed take on toddler aggression. (In fairness to previous researchers, discerning the motivations of toddlers is difficult, as they aren't terribly verbal.) It turns out that when toddlers are aggressive, they're often trying, however awkwardly and vainly, to balance their competing drives for autonomy and connection. They try, with violent assertions of their autonomy, to get others to see their hurt, disappointment, sadness, or frustration. If the parent or sibling who is the object of the aggression understands that the toddler is hurt, disappointed, sad, or frustrated, the connection will become more secure. As a result, most toddlers want affection soon after a temper tantrum that might include violence. It's not so much training in social rules that alters aggressive behavior as learning through experience that such behavior is unlikely to garner the compassionate response they really want.

Adults who get stuck in their Toddler brains under stress still act as if they can achieve a stronger connection by being aggressive or critical or vindictive. They inevitably hurt each other when they really want compassion, demand submission when they really want cooperation, and insist on "validation" when they really want connection.

Sometimes adults are aware of the hidden benign intention of Toddler brain aggression:

- "I wanted her to know what it feels like to be betrayed. Now we can start over."
- "If he doesn't feel really bad, there's no way he'll understand how he hurt me."

But most of the time, there is no intention to hurt when adults in the Toddler brain use criticism or shaming behavior to elicit compassion. Toddler brain shame-invoking statements like, "How can you live with yourself, treating me like you have?" are intended to draw out caring behavior that will strengthen the connection. Like toddlers, they attribute the negative response to their criticism and shaming as proof that others don't "get them." Instead of using Adult brain activities—reflecting on their behavior and reconceptualizing—they feel *justified* in continuing to use verbal coercion to get cooperation and to make others feel bad in the vain hope that their own pain will then gain sympathy and connection. Feeling justified makes them continue to do it even though they are smart enough to realize that it won't work.

The motivation to seek compassion, cooperation, and validation is so important that we'll consider how each is distorted in the Toddler brain.

Compassion in the Toddler Brain

Compassion literally means "to suffer with." It includes sympathy for the pain, discomfort, or hardship of another, with a strong motivation to help. Toddlers are able to experience the biological substratum of compassion as they attune their emotions to those of family members—when you feel bad, they feel bad. But they don't know what makes you feel bad or how to help. They want to give comfort, but worse than not knowing how, they see the urge to give comfort as a challenge to their autonomy. If they get too close to the hurt parent or sibling, they'll lose control of their own feelings. Without the Adult brain boundaries of personal identity, they become easily overwhelmed by the distress of others.

Adults in the Toddler brain have the same dread of compassion. They often see the pain and distress of others as a bottomless pit that will suck them in if they get too close. Just as bad, they see compassion as a threat to their autonomy; if they feel it, they'll have to submit. Yet they have no chance of balancing the drives for autonomy and connection without experiencing compassion for others.

Compassion vs. Submission

The Toddler brain struggle for autonomy makes it hard to distinguish compassion from submission. Experiencing someone else's discomfort feels like giving up the self. They won't know who they are if they let themselves feel what you feel. ("I can't be me if I'm feeling you.") Or if they let themselves feel the distress of others, they will have to do something they don't want to do. (For example, if I recognize that my coworker is not well, I might have to do his work. If your teenager acknowledges that you're exhausted, he might have to do the dishes for you.) Compassion feels like submission in the Toddler brain, because toddlers cannot appreciate the inherent rewards of cooperation.

Cooperation is *willingly* doing something to accomplish mutual or group goals or promote relationship harmony. Examples are doing your fair share on a rush project at work, helping the kids with their homework, or keeping the home a little neater than you might do if you lived by yourself, just because the neater home increases the harmony of the household. While humans hate to submit, we have a built-in reward for cooperation. This derives from a genetically transmitted trait that is even more important to survival in a highly complex social structure than it was in the dramatic struggles of early human history. Without cooperation, the meaning of our lives today would be reduced to trying not to get run over while crossing the street.

In the Toddler brain, the chances of effectively cooperating or gaining the cooperation of others are remote. Confined to a prison of self-obsession, adults in the Toddler brain interact with others from a position of implicit entitlement and coercion: "I have a right to get you to do what I want, and you will do it or else." Who wants to associate, much less cooperate, with that attitude?

In the Adult brain, we know intuitively that people are likely to cooperate when they feel valued and resist when they feel devalued. If you want cooperation, you must show value. If you want resistance, all you have to do is devalue—criticize, demand, act morally superior, or otherwise show ill will, as adults in their Toddler brains are wont to do. But don't think about *showing* value; that can smell of manipulation, even if you do it in the Adult brain. Focus instead on *feeling* value for other people. That means caring when someone is in pain or distress—showing compassion—*and* looking for something of value in the person, the interaction, or the relationship.

Adults in the Toddler Brain Use "Compassion" to Manipulate

I get many e-mails from people complaining that they were compassionate in their relationships, as I advocate, but that "it didn't work." What they mean is that, after showing compassion, they still didn't get what they wanted. Being kind or compassionate to someone so they'll behave the way you want or do something for you in return is an investment, not compassion. Like all investments, it's risky.

The use of compassion to cajole someone into changing is especially tragic in abusive relationships, when abused partners are desperate to bring about change. Their desperation is misconstrued by abusers as pure manipulation, to which they respond angrily and often abusively. Compassion is a healing emotion for the person who behaves compassionately because it engages Adult brain power to access our deepest humane values. But it's helpful to recipients only when they are in the Adult brain. The Toddler brain does not receive compassion positively. If you're in an abusive relationship, you must understand that your compassion will change you by putting you more in touch with your humanity, but it will not change your partner. Only your partner's compassion for you will change him or her.

Adult Brain Compassion vs. Toddler Brain Guilt

Adults in the Toddler brain are capable of guilt and remorse about hurtful or offending behavior. But those painful emotions lead to corrective behavior only in the short run. Guilt and remorse eventually produce resentment, anger, or abuse, as they are inevitably blamed, in the Toddler brain, on those stimulating the guilt and remorse. This happens when the discomfort of the emotions keeps us focused on how bad *we* feel rather than helping the people we offended feel better. The toddler who pulls his sister's hair resents her for crying because it makes him feel bad. Having inflicted abuse, adults in the Toddler brain are likely to rush their victims into fully trusting and forgiving them: "Get over it, so *I* can feel better."

To understand how unregulated guilt virtually guarantees recidivism, think of one of the most common types of guilt people feel in America today—not spending enough time with their kids. (Parents now spend an average of just thirteen minutes a day in task-free interactions with their children.) Does the guilt that most parents feel motivate them to be sweeter and more loving to their children, or does it make them more tense and irritable? Do they spend what little time they have striving for quality interactions with their kids or trying to control them? Feeling overwhelmed by their guilt, do parents back off emotionally and let their children do whatever they want?

Adult Brain Compassion vs. Toddler Brain Validation

Another major inhibitor of compassion is the Toddler brain's perceived need for validation. *Emotional validation* is understanding and expressing acceptance of another person's emotional experience. Young children certainly need parents to validate their experience, as the emerging sense of self is fragile and unable to reconcile thoughts and feelings with what is happening around them. But in most interactions between adults, validation is more complicated than what parents need to give to their toddlers. In adult interactions, validation must be mutual and respectful of differences in perspective.

In my long practice, I have never seen an adult who was resentful about not feeling validated by others, who was in the least interested in validating anyone's experience that differed from his or her own perspective. In fact, adults in the Toddler brain are more likely to *invalidate*—reject, ignore, or judge—other people's experience when they decide that it differs from their own. (In reality, people always have different experiences, as we'll see later. But adults in the Toddler brain often fool themselves by projecting their experience onto others.)

Adults in the Toddler brain are especially prone to confusing the desire for emotional validation with a drive to be perceived as right, even if it means making others wrong. This is a terrible curse in close relationships, because it drains them of compassion: "I don't care that you're hurt because you're wrong." Having to be seen as "right" justifies criticism, disrespect, and contempt in their eyes. It also requires an *illusion of certainty*. They have to be certain to prove that they're right.

Feeling certain is Nirvana to the Toddler brain in its struggle for autonomy. Adults who get stuck in the Toddler brain always opt for a simplistic emotional state that drowns out nuanced and often ambiguous intellectual analyses. (The Toddler brain simply cannot tolerate ambiguity.) But the emotional state of certainty is really a kind of intellectual illusion. To create a feeling of certainty, the brain must filter out far more information than it processes, increasing its already high error rate during emotional arousal. In other words, the more certain we feel, the more we're probably oversimplifying. The more certain we feel, the more likely we're wrong in some respect.

High-adrenaline emotions, particularly anger and fear, create the profoundest illusions of certainty due to their amphetamine effects. Amphetamines create a temporary sense of confidence, making you feel like you can do anything. But they achieve exalted feelings of confidence by narrowing mental focus and eliminating most variables from consideration. That's why you feel more confident after a cup of coffee (a mild amphetamine effect) than before it. It's why you're certain of danger when you're afraid, that you're a failure or defective when you're ashamed, and that you're right—and everyone else is wrong—when you're angry.

Perhaps the most self-defeating of Toddler brain burdens is seeking to be validated without seeking to validate, which usually translates into needing to be right while making different perspectives wrong. Ironically, feeling validated brings only a brief sense of well-being, unless we're able to respond compassionately in return. If you feel a need to be validated, it's wise to ask yourself the following questions:

- When you feel validated, does the good feeling last for just a short time, followed by a down mood or emptiness?
- Do you have trouble understanding perspectives that do not match your experience?
- Are you uncomfortable when you learn facts that do not fit your perspective?
- Is it hard to experience compassion for anyone who doesn't validate you?
- Do you have an urge to devalue (or retaliate against) anyone who doesn't validate you?
- Do you have trouble tolerating disagreement?

If you answered "yes" to any of the above, it's time to shift your focus from Toddler brain validation to Adult brain empowerment and growth.

Habits of the Toddler Brain Ruin the Best Adult Intentions

It's understandable why toddlers impulsively hurt their parents to try to get compassion and improve connection. But why do adults, with a powerful prefrontal cortex, continually repeat the same mistake? The answer is simple. They fall prey to habits that were formed in real toddlerhood and reinforced over a lifetime, which is remarkably easy to do. The brain is exquisite when it comes to forming habits. You might say it's a habit-forming machine. Hopefully, the following discussion explains why habits dominate adult behavior.

A primary function of the human brain is managing and conserving energy. Habits—behaviors we do without thinking—occupy so prominent a place in human and animal behavior because they are metabolically cheap, that is, they consume relatively little conscious energy. The difference in mental exertion between a habit and a consciously decided behavior is hundreds of millions of multifiring neurons. In familiar environments, most of what we do is on autopilot, activating strings of habits that consume far less energy than consciously decided behavior. Each time we repeat the autopilot behavior, we strengthen the neural connections that activate it.

Highly reinforced neural connections—what we experience as habits—are really a series of smaller conditioned responses. (If the brain loves habits, it adores conditioned responses.) A *conditioned response* forms through the repeated association of two things, for example, "A" and "B." After several repetitions, the occurrence of "A" automatically triggers the occurrence of "B." Russian researcher Ivan Pavlov gained fame in the early twentieth century by conditioning dogs to salivate at the sound of a bell. He simply rang the bell before feeding them. After a few repetitions of getting fed immediately after the ringing of the bell, the dogs got the idea. Of course they didn't think, *Oh, the bell has rung, we are going to be fed!* They reacted automatically, on a visceral level, to the sound of the bell, which their central nervous systems had associated with getting fed. Pavlov called this phenomenon *classical conditioning*.

We now know that it's not just behaviors that become conditioned. Mental states—thoughts, perceptions, sensations, and feelings—condition other mental states. Feeling sad might make you feel lonely, become more sensitive to sound (like footsteps in the hallway), remember losing your puppy as a toddler, and so on. Feelings themselves can condition other feelings. In the Toddler brain, sadness might cause guilt, which might cause shame, which might cause anxiety, and that might cause anger, regardless of what is happening around us. It turns out that the vast majority of emotional experience is a series of conditioned responses. By the time we reach adulthood, everyone has accumulated standard, almost generic emotional responses to the environment that run pretty much on autopilot; we think, feel, and behave more or less the same in the same mental states and social contexts, over and over.

More recent research suggests that many, if not most, of our decisions are made prior to conscious awareness by invoking habits of decision making. That's one of the reasons diets ultimately fail. Before you know you're hungry, much less that you want a hot fudge sundae, you're already motivated to consume one. What's more, conscious control of habits is limited, because it requires the most easily exhaustible of mental resources: focused attention. As soon as we're tired or distracted, willpower breaks down and habit or conditioned impulse predominates. As researchers Wendy Wood and Aimee Drolet put it, when resources are limited, people are unable to deliberatively choose or inhibit responses, and they become locked into repeating habits. Attempts at conscious control of habits are usually too little too late. After eating the whole cake (because you've associated sugar and fat with certain mental states), you'll remember, "Oh, I should have had a V8!"

Most of the literature about changing habits centers on reducing the reward of the conditioned behavior or substituting another behavior for the reward. That approach is unlikely to work with most troublesome Toddler brain habits, which are really a matter of conditioned mental states that lead to other mental states. To appreciate the difference, consider the Toddler brain habit of lashing out when feeling devalued. One obvious reward of the behavior is a release of energy; when toddlers *feel* something, they need to *do* something. This has led many authors and therapists to substitute another behavior routine for the same reward. That misconception led to now widely discredited anger management techniques, such as striking a punching bag or a pillow when angry. Multiple studies have shown that such behaviors may produce some short-term relief by expending energy, but in the long run they make us angrier, as they reinforce the conditioned association of vulnerable feelings (e.g., guilt, shame, fear) with anger. Angry adults, those in the habit of retreating to the Toddler brain under stress, have conditioned numerous associations of various emotional states underlying anger, any one of which can start a string of conditioned associations that lead to the lashing-out behavior. For example, the shame of failure or inadequacy, the fear of harm or isolation, and a dread of powerlessness frequently become associated with a sense of being wronged and feeling justified in a retaliatory response. Domestic violence classes have been shown to be unsuccessful in reducing violence when they attempt to invoke guilt and remorse for abusive behavior. This accidentally reinforces the conditioned association of abusive behavior with remorse, with the remorse coming *after* the abusive behavior. That is, the remorse does not occur until after the abuse, just as memories of the healthier choice of food are not available until experiencing the shame for having eaten the whole cake.

Adult brain habits must change the association of the Toddler brain's vulnerable states—mostly shame, fear, and powerlessness—that motivate the aggressive behavior, whether the hidden intention is to get a sympathetic response from others or to achieve temporary feelings of power.

All of this is to say that the habit of retreating to the Toddler brain under stress, forged by the high intensity of Toddler emotions when there was no self-regulation available in the underdeveloped PFC, will undermine the most benign intentions, the finest hopes to improve relationships, and the best strategies to be successful at work.

It's important to understand that Toddler brain habits will not go away just by understanding how they work or through insight of how you developed them in the first place. Once a habit is entrenched, there is no evidence that it can be unlearned. Old rats put in a maze they have not seen since they were pups are able to negotiate its twists and turns, and they can actually do it more efficiently under stress, when they receive electric shocks from researchers. Habits probably never disappear, and they definitely rule under stress.

In the next chapter, we see how we let other people keep us stuck in the Toddler brain.

CHAPTER 6

How We React to a Jerk Like a Jerk

Principles of Emotion Interaction

Disappointment or discomfort seems like unfair
treatment to toddlers. Refusing them something they
want, disagreeing with them, or failing to make them
more comfortable feels like utter rejection, stirring an impulse to
strike back. They can only assert autonomy by saying, "Mine!"
and "No!"

When disappointed or irritated, adults stuck in the Toddler
brain react more or less the same way. Anything that precludes
an easy "No!" response, such as the ambiguities of modern living,

makes them feel mistreated. "How dare the world be uncertain and ambiguous!" They get resentful and regard their own unfair demands as justifiable reactions to an unfair world. Their identity veers toward the negative, that is, their reactivity tells them who they're *not*, but they're never quite sure of who they are. Below is an example from my first session with a new client, whom I'll call "Jack."

"I agreed to have my brother-in-law, whom I don't like, move in with us, because my wife wanted it. I knew it wouldn't work out, but I went along, just to keep the peace. Now I keep noticing things about him that irritate me. I mean, it's one of those things where almost everything he does gets on my nerves. He snores, he doesn't comb his hair right. He bangs things around, plays his music when I'm trying to read, that kind of crap. I swear that sometimes he's *trying* to get on my nerves." Jack started to put his hand on the side of his face, but decided to use it instead for a broad gesture to underscore his complaint.

"And his sense of humor bites. He gets an attitude just because I make jokes about guys not getting jobs. I mean, they're funny jokes. This one I told was about this guy who's getting interviewed for a job, and the person doing the interviewing asks him, 'What's this you put under *disability*?' And the guy gets all defensive. 'I put *lazy*. What worse disability is there for working?'"

I smiled a little, but not enough to satisfy him. Although it would have given us some rapport, reinforcing his sarcasm with a laugh would have been a poor therapeutic choice. Perceiving rejection in my lack of amusement, he protested, "I work hard. I shouldn't have to put up with this crap in my own house. So I take it out on my wife—if it wasn't for her, I wouldn't have to put up with him. She knew I didn't want him there. She knew I just went along to keep the peace, because I didn't want a big argument." He grew quiet for a moment before admitting what he thought was a deep secret. "I'll tell you, if something bad doesn't happen to me, I'll find a way to make it happen. That's who I am."

Having his brother-in-law move in turned out to be a bit more complicated than Jack imagined when he agreed to it. In the face of complexity, he reverted to Toddler brain negative identity ("No!"), obscuring his deeper value of love and support for his wife. His behavior at home became one long pout, with only two emotional states: resentment or numbness. To avoid feeling numb, he looked for things to resent, such as his brother-in-law's snoring and choice of hair styles. Like so many of my clients, he sought out talk shows, political forums, and social issues that stirred his resentment or anger, just to feel more alive. The treatment for Jack, like most of my clients, was training him to access his Adult brain under stress. In the Adult brain, conviction, passion, and fidelity to deeper values make us feel more alive.

Not surprisingly, negative identity like Jack's—and any adult who gets stuck in the Toddler brain—yields an excess of negative feelings. When they cannot regulate negative feelings internally, people tend to seek external regulation; someone else has to calm them down and cheer them up, as we do for toddlers. Failure to

regulate one's internal experience—be it digestion or emotions—
raises the intensity of interactions. They'll appear needy (if they
need validation to feel okay) or like jerks (if they need to think
they're better than others to feel okay about themselves). With a
fragile sense of self depending on the outcome, all interactions
take on the form of, "I'm not okay unless you do what I want"
("Mine!"), to which the Toddler brain response will always be,
"I'm not okay if I do what you want" ("No!"). The higher stakes
placed on interactions increase the likelihood of staying stuck in
the Toddler brain, as we react to the negative way that others react
to us. If you react defensively when other people are defensive,
where will that get you? If you react to a jerk like a jerk, what does
that make you?

A sure way to get stuck in the Toddler brain is to want other
people to regulate your negative emotions for you. You'll almost
always get a negative response, due to the irresistible force of two
principles of emotion interaction: *reciprocity* and *contagion*.

Principle One: Emotion Reciprocity

"Doing unto others as you would have them do unto you" is
more than a virtue; it's the only way to have positive interactions.
That's because people tend to react in kind to the emotional states
they encounter. Psychologists call this principle *emotion reciprocity*. Because most emotions are either positive, increasing the
value of your experience, or negative, decreasing the value of your
experience, emotion reciprocity goes both ways. If you approach

a person—or a social animal, for that matter—with positive emotion, such as interest, curiosity, enjoyment, compassion, and so on, you're likely to get a positive response. (Not always, of course; sometimes people respond negatively to positive gestures because they're distracted, uncomfortable, tired, hungry, depressed, anxious, or stuck in the Toddler brain.) The other side of the reciprocity coin is called *negative reactivity*. If you approach someone negatively—with resentment, anger, demands, disrespect—you're even more likely to get a negative response. On autopilot, people are especially negative when interrupted or uncomfortable, tired, hungry, depressed, or anxious. Sometimes folks are able to soar above negative gestures directed at them, as we'll learn to do later in the book. But without deliberate effort in the Adult brain, emotion reciprocity rules.

Caring tends to prompt caring:

- "I feel bad that you're hurt."
- "That makes me feel better. And I feel bad when you're hurt, too."

Anger creates power struggles:

- "You have to do what I want."
- "No, *you* have to do what *I* want!"

And resentment breeds resentment:

- "I don't care about how you feel [the implication of resentment], but you *must* care how I feel."

This is certain to get a like response:

- "Why should I care about how you feel when you don't care about how I feel?"

When in the Adult brain, we're all smart enough to know that negative gestures rising from blame, denial, and avoidance are almost certain to make any interaction worse. But in the Toddler brain, negative reactions from others only reinforce perceptions of unfairness. Here's an example that frequently occurs in couples just starting treatment. Typically one of them had read on the Internet or in self-help books, or learned from a previous therapist, certain "communication skills." It would come so early in the session that they must have planned to say something like, "I don't feel supported," or "I feel judged." They then feel abused by the inevitable negative response from their partners. They were bound to get a negative reaction because they were behaving negatively, despite the careful choice of "I statements." They were still blaming; the subtext of such statements—what actually gets communicated—is, "You're making me feel bad by judging me or not supporting me." The negative reaction to their accusations only reinforced their perception of unfair treatment, making them feel like victims.

I chose this kind of example—"I feel judged; I don't feel supported"—because it's a common mistake. Adults in the Toddler brain are likely to confuse reporting or expressing a feeling with making a judgment about the intentions of others. Because we all have a right to our feelings, they seem to believe that putting their judgments in terms of feelings will seem less accusatory than stating what they think, as in, "I think you're judging me and not supporting me." Of course, it isn't. Toddler brain blame often comes in the guise of adult-sounding phrases and "communication techniques."

The coping mechanisms used to manage emotions are also subject to the principle of emotion reciprocity. Below is a matrix of the only possible interactions when both parties are in the Toddler brain.

Matrix of Toddler Brain Interactions

You	Other
Blame	Blame
Blame	Deny
Blame	Avoid
Deny	Blame
Deny	Deny
Deny	Avoid
Avoid	Blame
Avoid	Deny
Avoid	Avoid

The matrix shows why you go around in circles in Toddler brain interactions. The content of the interactions—whatever you're trying to talk about—*does not matter* when the principle of emotion reciprocity is violated. Introducing "facts" or "evidence" will be construed as more blame, denial of responsibility, or avoidance of the real emotional issue, which is usually a devaluing, superior, or dismissive tone. Emotion reciprocity will nail you every time you fail to understand other people's perspectives.

Always obscured in toddler coping mechanisms are the vulnerable emotions prompting their use. For example, "I'm sad" or "I'm ashamed" is more sympathetic than blame and more likely to invoke a sensitive response or at least a less defensive one.

Principle Two: Emotion Contagion

Did you ever think of how we know what they mean on the news when they say things like, "the mood of the nation," or "the feel of the community," or "you can feel the excitement in the air!" These metaphors make no *literal* sense. Yet we understand perfectly what they mean, thanks to our intuitive awareness of emotion contagion.

The principle of *emotion contagion* holds that emotions of two or more people converge and are passed from person to person in larger groups. Although we tend to think of them as purely internal phenomena, emotions are more contagious than any known virus and are transmitted subliminally to everyone in proximity. You're probably aware of how the emotional states of family members affect you; it's impossible to be happy when they're down and almost impossible to ignore their "attitudes" without some degree of defensive resentment or numbness.

Emotion contagion works even when there is little or no affiliation. Even in a crowd of strangers, emotion contagion makes us feel what the rest of the group feels. Experiments show that we're more likely to get impatient at a bus stop if other people are acting impatiently. But we're more likely to wait calmly if others seem resigned to the fact that the bus is late. And it's why the "electricity in the air" gets you excited at a sporting event or political rally, even if you were not particularly interested in the outcome, and you just went to be with a friend.

To understand the power of emotion contagion, you only have to consider its survival advantage. Sharing group emotions gives us multiple eyes, ears, and noses with which to sense danger and opportunity. Hence it's common to all social animals—packs, herds, prides, and, in the case of early humans, tribes. When one member of the group becomes aggressive, frightened, or interested, the others do, too. Witnessing the fear or distress of another person in a group can easily invoke the same emotional state within us. Happy people at a party make us happy, caring people make us care, the interested attract our interest, and the bored bore us. We avoid those who carry chips on their shoulders and those who bring us down or make us anxious.

Like anything that affects emotional states, contagion greatly influences thinking. Opinion pollsters know that they get one set of responses to questions they ask of people in groups and another when they ask the same questions of individuals in private. It's not that folks are lying when in a group or that they change their minds when they're alone. It's more accurate to say that, at least on some issues, they have different public and private minds, due to the influence of emotion contagion.

The principle of contagion also accounts for groupthink, which makes people apt to conform to the majority at a meeting or to act collectively against their own better judgment. The high-risk behavior of teen gangs occurs as emotion contagion spurs kids to move beyond, sometimes far beyond, their personal inhibitions into dangerous, cruel, or criminal behavior. Similarly, corporate and governmental scandals reveal how otherwise good people can get swept up in a frenzy that overrides their personal morality. Emotion contagion produces solidarity parades, protest marches, and, on the ugly side, "mob justice," lynching, riots, and looting. On a less dramatic level, it gives us constantly changing fashions, cultural fads, and political correctness.

Negative Emotions Are More Contagious

Did you ever wonder why people are more likely to notice things that stir negative emotion than those that might invoke a positive response? I'm not talking about the "negative people" who constantly look for the possibility of a dark cloud somewhere amid silver linings. Everyone gives disproportional weight to the negative. Consider how much you think about positive experiences compared to negative. Which consumes more time and energy running through your mind?

Emotions have what psychologists call *negative bias*. Negative emotions get priority processing in the brain because they're more important for immediate survival. They give us the instant adrenaline jolt we need to avoid snakes in the grass and fend off saber-toothed tigers, at the cost of noticing the beauty of our surroundings. Negative bias is why loss causes pain disproportionately to the joy of equivalent gain. Having a nice meal is enjoyable, but, in most cases, incomparable to the distress of missing a meal altogether. Finding $10,000 will be pleasant for a day or so; losing $10,000 can ruin a month. More poignantly, having a child is a joyous occasion (at least until fatigue sets in); losing a child takes a lifetime of recovery.

In relationships dominated by the Toddler brain, the negative bias of emotions makes it unlikely that I'll notice all the things people do that benefit me; appreciation is the province of the Adult brain. But I'll surely resent when they don't do what I want. In family relationships, research shows that it typically requires at least five positive gestures to counterbalance one little negative remark.

Ironically, positive emotions are more important to long-term well-being. You'll live longer and be healthier and happier if you experience considerably more positive emotions than negative ones. Life is better for those who are able to appreciate the beauty of the rolling meadow and the sun dappling the edges of surrounding trees, as long as they are able to notice the snake in the grass. We have to survive the moment to appreciate the world around us.

The negative bias of emotions profoundly affects emotion contagion. Even low-grade defensive/aggressive states like resentment spread relentlessly from person to person. If someone comes into work with resentment, by lunchtime everyone around that person is resentful. Aggressive drivers make other drivers aggressive. A hostile teenager ruins the family dinner, an impatient spouse makes TV viewing tense and unpleasant.

Emotional Pollution

The rapid, largely unconscious transmission of defensive or aggressive emotions such as resentment has created a kind of emotional pollution that keeps us locked in the Toddler brain. The psychological equivalent of litter and secondary smoke, emotional pollution is the display of defensive or aggressive emotions in the environment, in complete disregard of their adverse effects on others. The most casual contact with emotional polluters can make you feel ignored, defensive, impatient, self-righteous, sullen, or depressed, with no clue of the source of those feelings. If you encounter emotional pollution at work or on the street, you're not likely to be so loving to your family when you get home but are likely to blame your negative feelings on them. If you get into it with your spouse or kids before you leave the house in the morning, you're likely to drive aggressively or carelessly on the way to work and be in a sour mood once you arrive. Emotional pollution passes cubicle by cubicle throughout the workplace, car by car down the road, locker by locker in school, and room by room at home. Worst of all, if you're exposed to enough emotional pollution, you're bound to start spreading it yourself, unless you develop strong self-regulation skills: the ability to stay in the Adult brain amid a world of toddlers.

It's easy to understand why an aggressive emotion like anger would be so contagious. Our brains are constantly scanning the environment for threats to safety, and anger is a way to warn others not to mess with you. But the vast contagion of a more defensive emotion like resentment might seem harder to fathom, until you consider its duration and inherent self-deception. Resentment lasts a long time relative to other emotional states, including anger, so it has more time to spread to more people. More important, we don't conceal resentment as successfully as other emotions. Resentful people perceive no need to hide their resentment, as they might choose to do with their anger. That's because resentment feels very different on the inside than it looks on the outside. To see what I mean, try this experiment, especially if it seems as if no one understands you or cares about what you think or how you feel, and you can't figure out why.

- Look in the mirror for about a minute. (It takes that long to stop posing.)
- Close your eyes and think of something at home or work that stirs resentment. Think of how unfair it is and how it shouldn't be that way and you shouldn't have to put up with it. Continue to think about the incident or series of events in as much detail as you can.
- Now abruptly open your eyes, still thinking about whatever you resent, and you'll see what the world sees.

The world does not see the unfairness, hurt, or betrayal you feel inside. It sees only the resentment you display, which seems unfriendly, rejecting, even mean. If you feel that nobody truly gets you or appreciates where you're coming from, you may well be guilty of some form of emotional pollution that inevitably influences the way people react to you.

The hidden effects of emotional pollution can be more harmful to your well-being than taking in someone else's cigarette smoke and more aesthetically disquieting than stepping over other people's trash. Think of how much overreaction you see in the course of typical day—while driving, in stores, at work, at home, and in the media. I'm not talking about dramatic flare-ups. Think of the number of people you see who are not quite attuned to the moment and seem to bring emotion from somewhere else to the interaction you're observing . . . and what you see is just the tip of the iceberg. Most of the effects of emotional pollution are unconscious, processed by the brain in thousandths of a second. For every overreaction you consciously perceive, there are thousands more subdued displays of negativity. These can be scowls, impatient grimaces, vacant stares or looks of disgust, superiority, impatience, resentment, anger, or intolerance—so subtle that you aren't consciously aware of them or of how often your body and mind have to put up defenses against them. And here's the really sad news: those very defenses—conditioned responses over time—are less likely to shield you from emotional polluters than to make you one of them.

If you're around a resentful, angry, sarcastic, narcissistic, petty, vindictive person, you are likely to respond in kind, at least in your head. Unless you put up a conscious effort to stay in the Adult brain, they will make you almost as negative as they are. That much may not be surprising. The more alarming point is that you're just as likely to respond in that same negative way to the next person you encounter, unless that person makes a special effort to be gracious to you. But if your well-being depends on other people making special efforts to be nice to you, in no time at all you'll become powerless over how you feel, and as a result, behave more impulsively. You'll become a reactaholic, with the experience of your life controlled by reactivity to emotional pollution in your environment.

One way to think of Toddler brain reactivity is resistance to the unconscious pull of emotional pollution. It can be obvious, as in, "I'm not putting up with your attitude!" Or it can be passive, like trying to ignore your spouse's feelings. Once again, the aspect of Toddler brain reactivity that makes it difficult to see, let alone change, is its illusion of autonomy and free will. You think that you're acting of your own volition, when you're merely reacting to someone else. As long as you're in the reactive mode of the Toddler brain, you'll react to negativity with negativity, react to jerks like a jerk, react to abuse with abuse. The Toddler brain struggle for autonomy makes us slaves to emotion contagion and reciprocity.

All of this means that behavior motivated by the Toddler brain prompts others to react in kind and pass those reactions onto others. If someone says something disrespectful at work or if you encounter a jerk on the drive home, you're not likely to be as nice to your kids as you might ordinarily be, and they are more likely to act out or try to ignore you in response. (More about this in Chapter 12.)

Person by person, we build a culture of toddlerhood and an Age of Entitlement.

CHAPTER 7

Anger in the Age of Entitlement

Living in the Wrong Part of the Brain

They called the time of my early childhood the "Age of Anxiety." In the 1950s, scientists churned out new forms of destruction measured in "megatons." We practiced crouching under school desks, heads covered with bony arms—a maneuver designed to keep us safe in a nuclear attack. We feared communism, demagogues, the "yellow peril," polio, genetic mutation, overpopulation, and juvenile delinquency. Our anxiety came from threats that were faceless, formless, and impersonal, hovering just outside the flickering gray lights of our new TV sets.

The national media touted a second Age of Anxiety after September 11, 2001, pointing out that people drank more, upped their medications, bought elaborate security systems, and more frequently visited therapists and places of worship. The causes of this new anxiety, like that of the 1950s, were also impersonal, formless, and pervasive but decidedly different. To understand the difference, recall your gut reaction to the color of the daily terror alert level during the Bush administration—the equivalent of making school kids hide under their desks to avoid nuclear destruction. Was your reaction to the terrorist threat level *anxiety* or *resentment*? Did you feel the government was trying to protect you or exploit you?

In fact, the anxiety in post-9/11 America was mostly hidden, because we had learned to cover it up with resentment. The formula for resentment is any vulnerable emotion—anxiety, guilt, shame, fear, and so on—plus *blame*. If you blame your emotional discomfort on someone else, you gain the temporary advantage of self-righteousness—"I'm right; you're wrong" ("Mine!" "No!"). You get a small dose of adrenaline that gives temporary energy and confidence, although the latter is due to the oversimplified thinking that comes with adrenaline.

The emotional state you are likely to see most in an ordinary day is some form of resentment—an "attitude," sense of entitlement, complaining, whining, criticizing, or devaluing. Our perceived threats are no longer formless and anonymous. They cut us off on the highway or disregard, overcharge, disrespect, or try to control us; they're unfair, inconsiderate, and incompetent.

What happened between the end of the Cold War and 9/11 that masked anxiety with a veneer of resentment? The Culture of Toddlerhood eased into our consciousness through the back door of innovation:

- Proliferation of media through additional networks, cable TV, and multiplex theatres
- The Internet
- "Reality" TV

These were fertilizers for the Culture of Toddlerhood. But the main nourishment came later, from constant mobile connection to the Internet and related media, including social media. No wonder that under stress we're apt to become like toddlers in a supermarket.

Toddler Brain Culture

Although most self-defeating emotional habits were initially formed in toddlerhood, they would probably do little damage were they not so vigorously reinforced by pervasive cultural influences. When an entire culture promotes living and loving in the wrong part of the brain, we can hardly escape toddler dialogues of "Mine!" and "No!" or ignore politicians who sound like stubborn toddlers overstimulated by a twenty-four-hour news cycle. Nor can we elude continual power struggles, overreactions (temper tantrums), and resentful pouting, which make us respond with powerless frustration or, worse, react in kind.

Many factors contribute to the Culture of Toddlerhood. Below
are the chief ones:

- Entitlement (ever-expanding perception of "rights"
  and demands)
- Self-obsession (inability to see perspectives that go beyond
  personal experience)
- Splitting (good or bad, angel or demon, all or nothing)
- The cult of feelings (elevation of feelings over values)
- Intolerance of disagreement and uncertainty
- Substituting power for value (reacting to diminished
  self-value with exertion of power)

Entitlement

Though far from perfect, developed societies are now more
egalitarian, with more individual rights shared by wider and more
diverse segments of populations than ever before in human history. If our culture was dominated by the Adult brain, it would
marry the emergence of more rights with greater responsibility,
in recognition that the two are morally inseparable. For example,
we have a right to vote and a responsibility to learn as much as
we can to make an informed decision, based on the best interests
of the community or country. We have a right to speak and a
responsibility to listen. We have a right to argue and a responsibility to observe personal boundaries. In fact, all our rights entail
the responsibility to respect the rights of others. Yet the Culture of

Toddlerhood places so much emphasis on rights and entitlement ("get your needs met") that it divorces rights from responsibility.

Without responsibility, the perception of rights swells to a sense of entitlement—the belief that you have the right to do or get something and that your right is superior to the rights of those with different perceptions. When you feel entitled, you're not merely disappointed when others disagree or fail to accommodate your presumed rights; you feel cheated and wronged. The "unfair" response of others provides a stronger sense of entitlement, now with demands for compensation: "You owe me!" ("Mine!"). Of course, once you're older than four and not so cute anymore, the world is unlikely to meet your entitlement needs. Adults in the Toddler brain fall into a downward spiral. The more they don't get what they think they deserve, the more justified they feel in demanding compensatory privilege, also perceived as "rights." The person who cuts in front of you in line is often saying, "With the way I've been treated, I shouldn't have to wait in line, too!" Not surprisingly, criminals, domestic violence offenders, emotional abusers, and aggressive drivers have been shown in research to have a strong sense of entitlement.

Entitlement, Stress, and Anger in the Culture of Toddlerhood

It's no accident that the new sense of entitlement engendered by the Culture of Toddlerhood corresponds with the sharp increases in anger, resentment, and stress, which some researchers describe as epidemic. The more rights we perceive to be free of responsibility, the more we're bound to perceive that those rights are being violated. The mere possibility of rights infringement causes anger and stress.* If you think you're stressed all the time, thank the Culture of Toddlerhood for stimulating survival-level responses to petty ego offenses.

It's easier than you might think to construe ego offenses as survival threats. To begin with, the anger and stress hormones stimulated by ego injury are the same components of the primitive *fight/ flight/freeze* reflex common to all mammals. Activation of fight/ flight/freeze requires a dual perception of threat and vulnerability. When they are more vulnerable—exposed, wounded, starving, sick, or recently traumatized—animals respond to lesser threats with greater anger, fear, or submission. The activation of fight over flight/freeze is determined by the perceived annihilation potential of the threat. A raccoon will ferociously fight a rat to defend her newborn kits but not a cougar. More anger is observed in powerful animals, which tend to be predatory. Powerful animals use anger to acquire and defend territory and resources, thereby reducing threats to survival.

Fight, Flight, Freeze, and the Ego

Social animals, whose limbic systems differ little from that of toddlers, have to make choices about where to go, when to sleep, who eats what and how much, and who mates with whom. Lacking sophisticated language to negotiate and collectively strategize,

---

* It takes passion and commitment to achieve rights, but these give way to anger and aggression when the rights we already have seem violated.

the pack must develop some kind of executive function to make choices. Most social animals, including humans, answer this challenge by organizing into hierarchies, in which individuals achieve rank. Ascending up the hierarchy increases status, along with access to resources, with the most status and resources bestowed on a chief executive: alpha males or matriarchs. To establish rank and executive function, social animals invoke the old fight/flight/ freeze reflex. Since the threat of annihilation is lowest for the more powerful animals, they can afford more anger in competition for the top of the hierarchy. For the less powerful, submission or flight makes sense. In social animals, anger goes to the powerful, fear and submission to the less powerful. (Humans typically experience the submissive impulse as shame.) We know that the central nervous systems of all animals seek equilibrium; they can take just so much anger, fear, and shame. Solitary animals achieve equilibrium by isolation, social animals by acceptance of their place in the hierarchy.

With the development of the prefrontal cortex in humans came self-consciousness and the incorporation of status into the emerging sense of self or ego. Humans became creators of value. Status was no longer merely a means of access to resources, it became a separate entity, a "value of the self." This new estimation of the self as important brought with it a sense of entitlement to receive value from others, in the form of social approval (respect and admiration), as well as larger shares of resources.

Throughout the vast majority of human history, individual ego among the masses was suppressed by powerful members of the hierarchy through the use of force, dogma, and tradition. Only chiefs, kings, noblemen, priests, husbands, and parents could have big egos, assert entitlement, and express anger. What we call "human rights" began a slow emergence a few hundred years ago. But in the last sixty years the trend has accelerated sharply toward more enlightened, egalitarian cultures. We now recognize that everyone has equal value. Children are as valuable as parents; wives are equal to husbands; ordinary citizens are equal to heads of state; dark-skinned and light-skinned, patients and doctors, educated and noneducated, unpublished and published writers . . . all are equally valuable and entitled.

Unfortunately, status and the sense of entitlement that go with it were incorporated into the development of ego so long ago in human history that it's difficult to imagine value in terms of equality, except in an abstract or philosophical sense. Although we know better in the Adult brain, we assume in the Toddler brain that our rights are superior to those of other people. The inevitable negative response from others stimulates more anger, resentment, rudeness, and stress hormones. When the vulnerable ego feels threatened, the expression of opinions becomes opinionated and analysis gives way to confirmation bias at best, or, at worst, to dogma.

The perception of entitlement has soared exponentially with the Internet. Blogs, e-mails, social media, and interactive platforms seem to make everyone's opinions equally valuable, without regard to facts, truth, or morality. To get attention, the entitled individual almost has to develop a "Mine!" and "No!" approach to everything. Polarization, fueled by Toddler brain splitting (all good or all bad, all black or all white), has taken over the media and, by extension, political discourse. Angry, resentful, contentious, and rude e-mails, blogs, and tweets—like heavily negative political campaigns and governmental gridlock—are certain to get worse until we change the Culture of Toddlerhood.

I doubt that humans will ever decouple status from ego and achieve a totally egalitarian culture or a significantly less rude Internet. But we can come closer by drawing self-value from fidelity to our deepest values, including a sense of basic humanity, which we explore later in the book. Then we'll require less status-embedded value from others. Our egos will become less vulnerable, and defending them will be less necessary. We'll learn from other perspectives and enjoy the accretion of knowledge yielded by disagreements about evidence, concepts, and use of language. We'll escape the endless iterations of toddler coping mechanisms that cause us to make the same rude, tiresome, and harmful mistakes over and over. We'll enjoy the benefits of a well-developed Adult brain with a strong sense of responsibility for regulating Toddler brain entitlement.

Self-Obsession

In the beginning of the reality-show era of television, the rampant self-obsession on display was probably just the result of real people (non-actors) *pretending* to be real people for the camera. Marketers quickly learned that over-the-top self-obsession attracts viewers. The rest is history, as life has a way of mimicking art. For a lot of people, it's cool to think and act like reality show characters who are as fascinated with themselves as toddlers staring at a mirror. Many of my clients have revealed in therapy that they imagine themselves on camera several times a day. In the Culture of Toddlerhood, we can easily make our lives into a series of reality shows and become trapped, like a deer in the headlights, by the glare of our imagined reflections.

It's been argued that part of the popularity of reality shows is due to a kind of negative modeling—we don't want to be as self-obsessed as the players who fill our various media screens. If this is true, it's just another form of Toddler brain reactivity. But for it to be true, we would have to discount the marketing research behind the commercials that finance these shows, all of which promote various expressions of self-obsession.

Ironically, the Culture of Toddlerhood fixates on happiness as a primary objective, when nearly all its messages are of self-obsession and "getting your needs met." As we'll see in a later chapter, research on happiness shows that self-awareness, balanced with mindfulness of the environment and meaningful interactions with others, bring happiness, while self-obsession destroys it.

Splitting

Toddler brain splitting is a binary, all-or-nothing way of experiencing the world. It casts others as all good or all bad, with no shades of gray. At work it can take these forms: "You're either for me or against me" (meaning complete agreement or submission) and "My way or the highway." In love relationships, it sounds like, "Sometimes I love you, sometimes I hate you."

The Cult of Feelings

Much of pop culture tacitly assumes that how you feel is who you are. We live in a "cult of feelings," where what we feel has become at least as important as what we do. Think of all the news interviewers who shove microphones in the faces of politicians, perpetrators, and victims alike to ask the overwhelming question, "How do you feel?" We give more importance to personal feelings than personal values and to expressing how we feel rather than doing what we deeply believe is right. Tragically, we're preoccupied with blaming negative feelings on others rather than healing the hurt that causes them. A hallmark of our toddler culture is victim identity. A plethora of media talk and call-in shows seduce us into prolonging feelings of injury to illustrate how badly others have treated us. Like lawyers for the plaintiff, we try to prove damages, as if our suffering would hold offenders accountable, or healing and growing would let them off the hook. The cruel cost of victim identity is a perception of the self as damaged, which lowers the likelihood of healing and growth.

The cultural reinforcement of entitlement, self-obsession, and the cult of feelings creates three self-perpetuating trends that damage the human. In the first, people perceive themselves as entitled to express every feeling they have, almost completely disregarding the effects on others, just as they felt entitled to litter a few decades ago and to smoke in public buildings a few years ago. The result is a culture that elevates superficial feelings over the deeper value of relationships. Negative feelings are almost always received more negatively than those expressing the feelings intend, especially in close relationships. ("I feel you're ignoring me" is bound to get a defensive response.) Because negative feelings are more contagious and prone to reciprocation than positive feelings, adults trapped in the Toddler brain will most likely get negative responses to their expressions of entitlement. In the fog of self-obsession, negative reactions to their negative expressions make them feel like victims, with the right to retaliate.

The second disastrous result of the entitlement/self-obsession cult of feelings juggernaut is that people now feel entitled not just to the pursuit of happiness, not even just to happiness, but to *feeling good* most of the time. If you don't feel good, something must be wrong with you or your relationships. This cult of feeling good has led many people to develop acute intolerance for the vulnerable feelings that are a necessary part of life and love. Worse, they feel entitled to demand that others regulate the discomfort they can't tolerate. "You *have* to make me feel good" has become the subtext of a great many interactions. In the Culture of Toddlerhood, feeling bad is no longer motivation to heal, correct, and improve. It's a violation of rights.

Intolerance of Disagreement and Uncertainty

Prong three of the hellish triad of entitlement, self-obsession, and cult of feelings is that so many people now perceive themselves to have the right to control what others think and say. This trend started out justly enough in attempts to combat plagues of racism, sexism, ageism, and so forth. But the Culture of Toddlerhood inflated it, first to political correctness then to the current state of utter intolerance of disagreement. Slapping an "ist" or "ism" on other people's thoughts and expressions gives us the right to dismiss what they say and devalue them personally. In the extreme, the wisdom of every author before the age of political correctness can be facilely disregard as some kind of "ist." I recently saw a post accusing an author of sexism for using the word *master*, which the commenter regarded as patriarchal. I suppose the commenter wanted millions of women to surrender the master's degrees they've worked hard to earn, so as not to contribute to sexism.

To justify the "right" to devalue, all we have to do is claim to feel "offended." In the Toddler brain, the easily offended have become "ismists," ever ready to blame others for the chronic resentment that comes from their inability to control what other people think, say, and do.

Intolerance of disagreement ultimately rises from the dread of uncertainty. If we can tolerate it, uncertainty drives us to learn more, accomplish more, and connect to one another; it will make us smarter and more compassionate, as long as we can tolerate it. But the Toddler brain cannot tolerate uncertainty, because it provokes too much anxiety. (What you don't know might offend you.) Experiments show that anxious people have a lower tolerance of ambiguity and are more likely to miss nuances of information and perceptions, not because they're less intelligent or less sensitive or more prejudiced, but because they are more anxious. Calm the anxiety and they do much better in all areas. All of us, at one time or another, have reacted to uncertainty not by learning and connecting, but by trying to pretend that it doesn't exist. Instead of viewing uncertainty as a useful friend, we vainly try to deny or avoid it with dogma, superstition, delusions, drugs, ego, attempts to control the environment and the people in it, perfectionism, and anger.

Life can be hard for those who cannot tolerate uncertainty. Reality simply won't cooperate with their conception of it. But life can also be exciting and filled with value for those who embrace its inherent uncertainty.

Substituting Power for Value

Much of the psychological suffering in the world comes from substituting power for value. When they feel devalued, many people mistake the decline in energy and well-being that results from a deflated ego with physical threat. The adrenaline and cortisol stimulated by physical threat, even when erroneously perceived, make them feel temporarily more powerful and primed to exert power, either overtly or passively. A lot of the excess cortisol typically blamed on "stress" comes from Toddler brain egos perceiving continual threat and insult.

TV and movie screens are rife with displays of aggression in response to petty ego offenses. You can hardly watch an episode of a drama, comedy, or reality show without seeing this type of aggression. Nowhere is there a model of what every person needs to know: when feeling devalued, we must do something that makes us feel more *valuable*, not more powerful.

To make ourselves feel valuable under stress requires that we systematically convert Toddler brain feelings into Adult brain values, the topic of the next chapter.

CHAPTER 8

How to Turn Toddler Brain Feelings into Adult Brain Values

The latest research on the neurobiology of emotions shows that the particular way they feel depends on where in the brain they're processed. The Toddler brain feelings that most commonly trigger self-defeating blame, denial, or avoidance are:

- Fear, with its motivation to freeze or shrink (become a smaller target).
- Anger, with its motivation to devalue or attack.
- Anguish (seemingly unbearable loss), with its motivation to yell, scream, or wail.

- Shame (unlovable, defective, inadequate), with its motivation to cover up or hide.

The same feelings that sound like urgent alarms in the Toddler brain become mere emotional signals via Adult brain reality-testing:

- *Fear becomes concern or caution*, which motivates research, planning, and preparation.
- *Anger becomes impatience or frustration*, which motivates stepping back to evaluate the methods used to accomplish the goal, modifying them when appropriate, and redoubling efforts to achieve the task.
- *Anguish becomes sadness*, which motivates incremental increases in value creation to fill the void of loss. (The paradigm example is recovering from grief over the loss of a loved one. The purpose of grief is to love again.)
- *Shame becomes disappointment.* (The experience of shame in the Toddler brain is paralyzing and disorganizing, which is why toddlers have temper tantrums; the adrenaline temporarily empowers them. But disappointment motivates self-soothing and self-care, sharpening old skills and acquiring new ones in order to be more successful. If the disappointment signal is about attachment, it motivates connecting to loved ones—being more compassionate, kind, supportive, and loving.)

The Adult brain is able to achieve the above by attenuating the Toddler brain tendency to view transient negative feelings as permanent conditions. "I have always felt bad and always will feel bad. I don't know what it's like not to feel bad. You always make me feel bad." In the Adult brain, negative experience is temporary; the future is always near: "This bad feeling will pass. Most of the time I feel okay, and I will again. Sometimes our interactions go wrong, and neither of us acts the way we would like. *I will try to do better.*"

The inability of the Toddler brain to see anyone else's perspective—"I feel shut out; you must be ignoring me. I feel empty; you must not care about me"—is transformed, as the Adult brain puts emotional signals into *social context*: "I'm frustrated, which means I'm hurt or anxious, so he or she must be hurt or anxious, too." "My partner is reacting to something different from my perception; I'll try to understand and sympathize with his or her perspective and communicate mine more clearly and respectfully." And, if ignored or rejected, "My partner must feel preoccupied or overwhelmed. I'll let him or her know how much I like feeling connected. If we can't connect right now, I'll create value in different ways, for example, by playing with the kids, talking to a friend, or writing a poem."

The ability of the Adult brain to put emotions in a social context can be developed like any other skill. I call it *binocular vision*, and I say more about it later.

Shifting from the Toddler Brain to the Adult Brain: Reality-Testing

Sophisticated reality-testing is a great advantage of the Adult brain. But habits of retreating to the alarm-driven Toddler brain under stress weaken this vital function. Here's an example of using the enormous power of the Adult brain to test reality, starting with the kind of Toddler brain expression I hear all the time in my practice:

"I feel shut out," one partner says to the other. Although "shut out" is not a feeling but an attribution about the intentions of others, the focus on the negative state nevertheless amplifies and magnifies it. The speaker will probably come off as needy, demanding, or resentful, any of which are likely to elicit a Toddler brain response from the listener.

An example of Adult brain reality-testing and regulation is, "Am I really shut out, or does it merely feel that way? What can I do to feel more connected?" Note that we validate the feeling, while recognizing that it's merely a signal about a possible reality. We're thus empowered to improve the experience rather than explain and justify it (which amplify, magnify, and prolong it). Now we're likely to choose behaviors that will enhance connection, rather than blame the feeling on our partners.

The formula for developing this habit is simple:

- *Think of a negative feeling at home or at work*, preferably one that escalated into an unpleasant encounter. Pretend it's happening now. Try to feel the physical sensations that go with the feeling: increased heart rate, stiffness in your shoulders, clenched fists, and so on.

- *State how you feel.* Use the deepest actual feeling—for example, "I feel inadequate," *not* the attribution about other people's intentions: "I feel they're disregarding me."
- *Apply Adult brain reality-testing.* "Am I really inadequate, or did it just feel that way? No, of course not. I've done lots of things well and competently" (think of specific examples). Or "If they're intentionally disregarding me, it's probably because they're preoccupied; I'll respectfully assert my position." Or "If they're really disregarding me, it's probably because they don't trust my input. I will work to earn their trust."

In short, always validate the feeling, test it against reality, and choose behavior that will improve your experience. (This is just an outline. I'll present a practice regimen for developing Adult brain habits in the next chapter.)

Accept and Improve

Adults stuck in the Toddler brain suffer the unmitigated cruelty of the "whys" and "shoulds." They spend most of their emotional energy trying to figure out *why* something happened, protesting that it *shouldn't* have happened, and insisting on what *should* have happened instead. Put another way, they waste mental energy on why they got into the hole and who's to blame for them being

there. Psychological suffering is greatly and unnecessarily prolonged when we become fixated on why something happened
or on protesting that it should not have happened. (The Buddha
said two and a half centuries ago that most of the suffering in
the world comes from wishing it were not the way it is.) Focus is
more wisely placed on developing skills to climb out of the hole
as well as habits to stay out of it. Once we accept the way things
are, we can channel all the emotional energy spent railing against
it into healing and improving. The mantra for soaring above is
accept and improve. (There will be more on "improve" later in
the chapter.)

I'm Disappointed, but I'm Okay

Research shows that toddlers stop having temper tantrums
when they develop an emotional vocabulary—when they're able,
for example, to say, "I feel disappointed." Research shows clearly
that the ability to label emotional states is crucial to efficient regulation of them. The Compassionate Parenting program I estab-
lished in the 1990s includes training for parents to teach emotional
vocabulary to young children. Although labeling emotional states
is an Adult brain activity, we have shown that toddlers can learn to
do it, albeit in the most rudimentary of ways. Here's a page from
the Compassionate Parenting manual to show how we do it with
toddlers. I think it makes a valuable point about shifting from the
Toddler brain to the Adult brain under stress:

The single most important emotional word for children to learn is "disappointed." Most of their intensely negative states are triggered by disappointment; they want something they can't have. Without the ability to regulate disappointment, the negative feeling can quickly spiral downward into an abyss of feeling unlovable-inadequate-defective. Feelings of unworthiness are overwhelming for toddlers because they smack of life-or-death. Remember, the only thing toddlers can do for their own survival is attach emotionally to someone who will take care of them. Unworthiness of attachment is unbearable. They empower themselves the only way they know how, with the adrenaline of a temper tantrum.

Parents cannot talk their toddlers out of that negative state, but they can teach them to put a floor under disappointment, to keep it from cascading into unlovable-inadequate-defective. When children can say, "I feel disappointed," they begin to have power over their emotions.

To teach emotional vocabulary to young children,

1. Pick a quiet time, preferably before reading a bedtime story;
2. Use an incident when the child experienced the emotion during the day;
3. Confine each lesson to five minutes or less;
4. Repeat the process for several nights.

The best time to teach emotional vocabulary is in bed, after you've tucked the child in and before you read to him or her. (It's always good to read at least a paragraph to your child every night.) Of course, you should tailor the following to the language capabilities of your child.

Parent: I want to talk about how you felt when we were in the grocery store today. Remember when you asked to have that candy, and I said, "No"?

Child: Yes.

Parent: Do you remember how you felt just before you got upset?

Child: No.

Parent: It looked like you felt disappointed. That means you wanted the candy [parent lifts arms and eyes, as if excited], you really wanted it! Then when I said, "No" [parent goes limp in a look of disappointment], you felt really down. You really wanted the candy [parent lifts arms and eyes, as if excited], then I said, "No" [parent goes limp in a look of disappointment]. Do you remember that?

Child: Yes.

Parent: Is that how you felt?

Child: Yes.

Parent: That feeling is called "disappointment." When we want something and can't have it or want to do something but need to do something else, we feel "disappointed." If that's how it was for you when you couldn't have the candy, can you say, "I felt disappointed"?

Child: "I felt disappointed."

Parent: Great! Try it again: "I felt disappointed."

Child: "I felt disappointed."

Repeat this process for several nights. Whenever you notice in the course of the day that your child is disappointed, point it out at the moment and ask him or her to say, "I feel disappointed." The ability to articulate, "I feel disappointed," puts a floor under the negative feeling so that it doesn't drop into an abyss of feeling unlovable, inadequate, or defective.

After you are sure that the child has this down, add the following:

Parent: Remember when you felt disappointed today? Well, we're going to add something to what you say. Can you say, "I feel disappointed, but I'm okay"?

Repeat the process above with, "I feel disappointed, but I'm okay."

Shifting from Toddler brain alarms to Adult brain values is very much like teaching emotional vocabulary to a young child, except that the adult teaches himself to recognize the current conditions of reality, accept them, and improve or transform them.

"I'm afraid" becomes "I'm concerned or cautious, but I'm okay, and I'll figure out the right thing to do, according to my deepest values—the things that are most important to me."

"I'm angry" becomes "I'm frustrated or impatient, but I'm okay, and I'll improve, appreciate, connect, or protect."

The urge to scream in anguish becomes "I'm sad at the loss, but I'm okay, and I will create more value—appreciate, connect, protect, improve."

"I'm ashamed" becomes "I'm disappointed, but I'm okay, and I'll learn more, work harder, do my best to be successful." If stuck in the Toddler brain in a love relationship, the way to the Adult brain begins with, "I'm disappointed, but I'm okay, and I love you. Together we can solve this."

Don't be discouraged if your feelings seem overwhelming—that is, you *don't* feel okay. Any difficulty you might have switching to the Adult brain when feelings are strong is just force of habit and not likely due to any emotional disorder (apart from the normal anxiety, resentment, and depressed mood resulting from Toddler brain habits). As I discuss in the next chapter, changing habits is a slow process that always feels awkward in the beginning. With practice, you'll gradually build the skill to shift into the Adult brain, where painful negative feelings are turned into valued-based motivations to heal, correct, and improve.

Toddlers Split, Adults Integrate

Our political landscape has been hijacked completely by Toddler brain splitting. Both sides of an issue can see only their own perspective; anything that departs from it is intolerable. We wouldn't ride in a plane designed by a toddler, yet we endure political strategies that appeal only to the Toddler brain. One thing is for sure: We won't get Adult brain politics as long as we support pandering to the Toddler brain's penchant for splitting and self-obsession, not to mention blame, denial, and avoidance. Our politicians won't grow up until we do.

Fortunately, the Adult brain is capable of integrating the positive and negative as *parts* of a whole. Good people make mistakes; respectable people disagree. We hold on to value for other people when we disagree with them or don't like their current behavior. (When no one feels devalued or defensive, negotiation and improvement are possible.) In the Adult brain we know that black-and-white issues are rare. We seek to shine light on the gray areas between us. The truth is almost always in the gray. So are lasting success and happiness.

For close relationships to flourish, we must be able to say, "I love you when I feel good and when I feel bad. I love you when you feel good and when you feel bad. I love you when I don't like your behavior. I love you when you don't like my behavior." Relationships dominated by the Toddler brain suffer emotional divorce with every bad feeling, every disagreement, and every differing behavior choice. In the Adult brain, the relationship is valued more than the points of disagreement. When the value of the relationship is honored, partners are motivated to integrate their perspectives in ways so that both can feel okay.

Of course, the Adult brain cannot integrate all concepts and emotional states, as the variations are too numerous and too complex. But it can—and must—keep all of them in proportion. Where the experience of negative feelings in the Toddler brain amplifies and magnifies only negative aspects of relationships and policies, the Adult brain sees them in a broader context—as individual colors on a larger palette. Some of the colors on the palette are useful, others enrich our lives, a few are just okay, some we don't like but can tolerate, and some need to change. Mindfulness of the palette as a whole lowers the amplification and magnification created by the Toddler brain's focus on the negative. It allows us to replace fixation on how bad things seem with a focus on values. Mindfulness helps us emphasize what we're for, rather than what we're against. It helps us soar above.

Seek to integrate, not reject.

The Path from Toddler Brain
Feelings to Adult Brain Values

Another great advantage of the Adult brain is the ability to reflect. It enables us to step back and think about who we are, how we are in the world, and what we want to do. The reflective process can be short—just a few minutes—or prolonged, as in a weekend or month-long retreat. Some evolutionary psychologists say that the need for reevaluation is one reason we tend to get depressed after loss or failure at work or at home. They cite the lower rate of metabolism and diminished sex drive characteristic of depression as evidence. Early humans were less able to find food or reproductive opportunities following loss or failure. This forced them into periods of reevaluation that lasted until they developed new strategies to succeed. In the Adult brain, we reflect and reevaluate after failure to develop new strategies or different approaches. We reflect and reevaluate after loss to marshal the mental resources necessary to create more value—to improve, appreciate, connect, and protect. We grieve in order to love again.

Reflection is limited to the current state of feelings in the Toddler brain; what they feel is the only reality. A neurological principle, which we'll call the *first neurological principle*, explains why reflection only makes things worse in the Toddler brain:

Mental focus amplifies and magnifies; whatever we focus on becomes more important.

The more we focus on a feeling or the presumed causes of it, the more important it becomes, making everything else in life less important. Moreover, focus on feelings does not reveal them so much as change them, in a kind of *Heisenberg effect*. The great physicist Werner Heisenberg discovered that the act of observation *changes* the object of the observation, creating uncertainty about what we're actually observing. When we reflect on feelings, they change, at least in intensity. For example, we tend to become more irritable if someone calls our attention to it. You're likely to feel disconnected from a spouse who asks if you feel connected. Thinking about your sadness can make you angry, and dwelling on worries can make you fearful. (Low-energy feelings almost always give way to those with higher adrenaline. If you want to feel bad, simply reflect on a small negative feeling and watch it grow.) Worst of all, when we focus on feelings, we become less aware of reality, just as focus on reality makes us less aware of feelings.

When we focus on how we feel, past instances that evoked similar feelings—loss, rejection, powerlessness, and a sense of injustice—are loaded into implicit memory. (Once again, this creates an illusion that it's always been that way, that we've always felt bad or mistreated and, by implication, it will always be this way.) If the feelings are painful, we'll only remember instances of pain and loss. If the feeling violates a deeper value, for example, hostility toward a loved one or a vengeful impulse to sabotage a project at work, it must be *justified*. The justification process appropriates the prefrontal cortex to look for evidence that will prove how the loved one *earned* your hostility or the project manager *deserves* to fail. For example, "I feel resentful. I have a right to feel resentment, because they did this, this, this, and this, not to mention that, that, that, and that. I put up with a lot over the years. This is exactly like what I had to put up with in the past—or not exactly, but close enough," and so on and on and on. If both parties in an interaction do this, whether at work or at home, they become prosecuting attorneys, arguing a case by cherry-picking supporting evidence, while ignoring all disconfirming facts. The only thing that reflecting on feelings reliably gets is self-obsession.

The *second neurological principle* should put the nail in the coffin of emphasizing feelings over values and behavior:

> *Neural connections forged by repeated focus grow physically larger and stronger and are prone to automatic activation. That is, repeated focus forms habits; anything we do repeatedly, we'll eventually do on autopilot.*

In other words, acting on feelings becomes a habit bound to make us repeat past mistakes over and over.

How Do I *Want* to Feel?

When it comes to feelings, the best strategy is to validate them (briefly) but put your focus on how you *want* to feel. This approach is more future-oriented and less susceptible to the feedback loop of past mistakes. More important, it invokes Adult brain values.

"I feel resentful, but I *want* to feel kind." With this subtle but crucial shift in focus, past experiences of feeling kind are loaded into implicit memory. I recognize that I really like myself better at those times, because kindness is part of my value system. I imagine myself doing things that will bring those feelings to life, such as wishing others happiness and well-being. I practice allowing myself to be concerned with the well-being of my loved ones. I practice behaviors that embody my concern for them.

A focus on how badly we feel and why we might feel that way locks us in the Toddler brain. Thinking of how we want to feel moves us to the higher functions of the Adult brain. There we more efficiently reconcile thoughts and emotions with perceptions of reality and choose behavior consistent with our deeper values. We soar above Toddler brain reactions.

Feelings vs. Values as Behavioral Guides

If you act on your feelings consistently, you'll certainly violate your values. Besides the fact that no one feels like being true to values all the time, feelings are stimulated by many things that run counter to values. Highlighting the differences between feelings and values should make the better motivational choice obvious.

Feelings are:

- Highly reactive to the environment;
- Greatly influenced by physiological states—metabolism, hormonal variations, hunger, thirst, and tiredness;

- Largely conditioned—activated by the vaguest of similarities with past experience, which is why those who act on feelings make the same mistakes over and over;
- Transitory. They come and go within a few minutes, provided you don't amplify, magnify, and prolong them by over-validating or justifying them.

In contrast, core values are:

- Far less reactive to the environment and more attuned to what is most important;
- Far less influenced by physiological states. You're not likely to stop loving or become less humane when tired, hungry, thirsty, or sick;
- More available to choice (less conditioned);
- Consistent over time—more or less permanent.

Feelings follow value investment, but not the other way around. If you allow your deeper values to motivate behavior, your feelings will follow. You'll feel more authentic, with a stronger identity and more coherent sense of self. If you act on your feelings, you won't know who you are, as who you are gets lost in the vicissitudes of transitory feeling states. Identity is reduced to whatever you feel at the moment.

How Toddler Brain Feelings Become Adult Brain Values

Like feelings, values have a motivational function. They tell us to do something. The behaviors that values motivate fall into four broad categories: *improve, appreciate, protect,* and *connect.* These are so important that each requires further explanation.

Improve

We function at our best when seeking to improve something. Just thinking about how to improve your situation or your experience engages large numbers of neurons in the prefrontal cortex and activates the positive—and usually productive—emotion of interest. The more interest we can summon, the more likely we are to improve, which is why we do so much better when interested in tasks than when we're bored with them.

Probably the greatest barrier to improving is the inability to fix something or make it 100 percent better. It's more productive to think of improving as an *incremental* process—making things *a little* better in each of several steps. In emotionally charged conditions, it's nearly impossible to go directly from feeling bad to 100 percent improvement. (It takes about twenty minutes for the most potent effects of cortisol to wear off.) But once you make something 10 percent better, it becomes easier to make it 20 percent better. Then it's easier to make it 40 percent better, and so on. Strive to make a bad situation a little better if you can, but if you can't, then make your *experience* of it better. For example, a common problem after divorce is the hard feelings of valued former in-laws. In this case, you would start out thinking of what might make the situation with, say, your ex-mother-in-law 10 percent better—perhaps sending her a sincerely written card or a flower would serve as an olive branch. If that—or anything else you try—doesn't improve the situation, change the way you experience it. In place of the self-denigrating interpretation that she's rejecting you, see her as a hurt woman trying unsuccessfully to deal with her own pain. That doesn't excuse her behavior, but it improves your experience of it. When we choose to control the meaning of our experience, we can soar above. When we don't choose to improve, we're likely to get stuck in the Toddler brain and repeat the same mistakes—and feel the same pain—again and again.

Below are the major types of *improve* motivations:

- Situational. Try to make the situation you're in more beneficial, productive, or convenient.
- Experiential. Try to make your experience more comfortable, pleasant, or pleasurable.
- Transcendent. If your experience remains negative, try to make your situation and/or experience less meaningful to you.

To see the power of the Adult brain in *improve mode*, try this exercise: Note your current emotional state. Count to five, then read aloud the following improve behaviors:

- Learn
- Grow

- Enhance
- Expand
- Analyze
- Build
- Repair
- Renew
- Redeem

After reading the above list aloud, note your emotional state for a second time. You should find a slight elevation, just from saying the words. Imagine the effect of enacting the behaviors.

Appreciate

We typically think of appreciation in terms of complimentary expressions like, "You're wonderful, special, awesome, smart, attractive, etc." Though they're sometimes nice to hear, expressions like these often feel hollow. That's because appreciation is primarily a felt condition, not a verbal one. Missing in most compliments is the essential component of appreciation—*opening your heart*—that is, allowing yourself to be enhanced by certain qualities of other people or things. For example, "When I appreciate how loving you are, your fine work, or your thoughtful gestures, I am enhanced, that is, I become a better person as long as I appreciate you." This is why appreciating and being appreciated are so appealing in relationships: both parties become better people. What's more, my appreciation of you has a ripple effect. It helps me appreciate the beauty of the sunset, the drama of the painting, or the excitement of the movie or play.

Appreciating helps us:

- Regulate negative moods
- Break the stronghold of autopilot functioning
- Give life dimension, dynamics, and color
- Maintain a sense of meaning and purpose
- Be happier
- Sustain intimate connection.

In general, you'll achieve more growth by finding something to appreciate in a difficult circumstance or relationship than in a benign one. For instance, Mia's mother was highly critical, covering everything from Mia's parenting style to her choice of makeup and dinner menu. It seemed that every encounter, by phone or in person, left Mia angry, initially at her mother then at herself for needing her mother's help with the financial crisis that resulted from the breakup of her marriage. In treatment, Mia learned to compassionately assert behavioral parameters (how she wanted to be treated), while appreciating certain qualities of her mother. For example, she always tried to help and truly wanted what was best for Mia.

As it turned out, Mia's mother was quite moved to learn that her only daughter truly appreciated her, which allowed her to hear and respond positively to Mia's assertion of how she wanted to be treated. But even if this kind of compassionate assertiveness had been unsuccessful—say that her mother got defensive and more critical—Mia would have gained the benefits of her compassionate efforts. Appreciation decontaminated most of her thoughts about her mother. Even if her mother remained critical, Mia would no longer hold on to the residue of their unpleasant interactions.

The ultimate issue isn't whether people deserve your negative thoughts; certainly many people do. The more important point is that they are *your* thoughts in *your* head, and you want them to be as beneficial to you as possible. We cannot appreciate and feel devalued at the same time. As long as you appreciate, you will not feel devalued, and you'll eventually soar above.

Protect

The creation of value carries a simultaneous instinct to protect the person or object of value. If you own valuable objects, you probably have some kind of security system in your house. If you love someone, you have an unconscious and automatic instinct to protect that person. The instinct to protect motivates a wide range of behaviors from the routine to the heroic. It will lead you to get reliable car seats for your children, and make sure they eat nutritiously, sleep well, and do their homework. It will also move you to risk your life to rescue them from danger. The formation of emotional bonds activates the most powerful instincts to protect.

We are not descended from the early humans who had little instinct to protect kin, because they perished and did not pass on their genes. The instinct to protect gave humans a distinct survival advantage over more numerous and powerful competition, such as big cats, wolves, and other hominids. The ability to protect emotional bonds facilitated mutual protection and sustenance, which led to a psychological melding of survival with emotional bonds. We not only bonded to survive, we survived to form bonds.

Protection is so important in modern times that genuine self-value (as opposed to narcissistic delusion) rises and falls on the ability to protect loved ones. We feel more valuable when we protect them and less valuable when we fail to protect them. Imagine the emotional fate of a world-class CEO who lets go of his child's hand in traffic to watch in horror as she runs to her death.

On the other hand, if you feel that you can protect your family's well-being, your self-value will be high, even if you fail in other areas of life. I remember the manager of our Little League baseball team who was beloved by his two sons and idolized by the rest of the kids. We could take any kind of personal or school problems to him for help and guidance. As I look back on his confident demeanor and compassionate behavior, I'm sure his self-value was high, due to his ability to protect the emotional well-being of his children and their friends. Yet our parents considered him a loser for working as a grocery store checker into his mid-forties and, worse in their eyes, seeming content with it.

To a large extent, the protective instinct attenuates misfortune. Research shows that getting fired from a job is easier on those more attuned to the protection of their families than their own ego. Protective people tend to search immediately for another job as a means of putting food on the table, while the ego-driven are likely to endure a few weeks of painful depression and drinking. It takes longer for them to recover because they misunderstand their pain, which is not telling them they are failures; it's telling them to protect their families. The pain will continue until they heed its message and resume protection of their families, at least emotionally if not financially.

Suppression of the instinct to protect ultimately diminishes the ability to love. Many people who feel like failures at protecting the well-being of their families are susceptible to sexual affairs, drug abuse, and a myriad of compulsive behaviors that ruin relationships.

Connect

Connection is a sense that some part of your emotional world is also part of someone else's. It's a transcendent state, in that it makes us rise above purely selfish and petty concerns to value the well-being of significant others or communities. On a biological level, connection elevates blood levels of the bonding hormone oxytocin, which makes us feel calm, safe, and secure.

Human beings require connection because:

- Our brains are hard-wired for it. We were never a solitary species; we're the most social of all mammals, forming the strongest and most enduring emotional bonds.
- We suffer physically and mentally from disconnection.
- We become psychotic without social cues. This happens to prisoners kept in solitary confinement too long and to some elderly who live alone and isolated.

Perhaps the most important thing to know about connection is that it's a mental state and a choice. You choose to feel connected to certain people or communities, and you choose to feel disconnected. The choice to feel connected can be independent of relationships, that is, you can feel connected unilaterally, as many people do when loved ones are estranged or deceased.

Research evidence suggests that human beings function at their best when investing in three levels of connection, although the amount of investment in each is rarely equal. That is, we tend to major in one, minor in another, and make minimal investment in the third.

The major levels of connection are as follows:

Intimate: Good friends, lovers, and family members. These are the most personal of emotional bonds, with the greatest amount of self-disclosure and commitment to the well-being of others. To thrive, intimate bonds require affection, unconditional safety and security for all parties, and relative freedom from resentment and hostility. They must feature at least some kindness and consistent compassion when loved ones are in pain, discomfort, or distress.

Collective or *Communal*: Investment in a group, where individual relationships are secondary to the concerns of the group. Collective connections provide crucial feelings of belonging and social identity. Research shows that feeling excluded from communal connections is one of the most enduringly painful of social conditions. In the past, communal connections evolved naturally in neighborhoods. But the steep decline in sense of community that has occurred all over the world in recent decades has largely confined collective connection to groups and organizations whose principles, values, goals, or interests participants agree to share.

On the positive side, collective connection gives us patriotism, faith-based communities, groups geared to civic causes and charities like Lions, Rotary, and Kiwanis, and youth development organizations such as the Boy Scouts and Girl Scouts and 4-H clubs. On the negative side, the need for a collective connection has produced fascism, cults, youth gangs, and groups dedicated to hatred and terrorism.

Transcendent: Helps us relate to something greater than the self, such as some notion of God, religion, morality, social causes, nature, the cosmos, or simply the vast sea of humanity. This sublime level of connection makes us aware that, even though we metaphorically stand on a lone rock looking up at the overwhelming infinity of a starry night, we are connected, in some mysterious way, to something greater. (The paradox of human nature is that we feel more significant when accepting our insignificance.)

We turn Toddler brain feelings into Adult brain values by activating instinctual motivations to improve, appreciate, protect, and connect. We make the final transition from feelings to values by expanding on "I'm disappointed, but I'm okay." It looks like this: "I'm disappointed, so I will improve, appreciate, connect, protect."

Developing *new habits* that help us improve, appreciate, protect, and connect, especially under stress, is the topic of the next chapter.

CHAPTER 9

Adult Brain Habits

Improve, Appreciate, Connect, Protect

Many if not most of the behaviors that cause failure and suffering are merely *habits* developed primarily in toddlerhood and reinforced throughout our lives. Changing them won't be easy. But the reward for the considerable effort required to do so will be nothing less than a better life. Changing habits changes the meaning of life.

Habits and Meaning

Higher-order prefrontal cortex operations make us occasionally reflect on the meaning of our lives. The greatest books of philosophy, religion, and literature engage the Adult brain to that end. But lower-order habits, many of which come from the Toddler brain, create our moment-by-moment experience. Our loftier thoughts about the meaning of life are like waves that rise and fall on a stream. Waves attract attention, but the stream goes where the current beneath the surface takes it. In human experience, habits are like the current beneath the surface. They direct the majority of our behavior and, therefore, determine the meaning of life by default. We can consciously decide what our lives mean to us, but to change the meaning, we must change our habits.

Habits of Creating Value vs. Habits of Exerting Power

It bears repeating: Most of the emotional distress people suffer —indeed, much of the abuse and violence in the world at large— comes from habits of substituting power for value. When they feel devalued, many people regress to the toddler habit of getting angry to feel more powerful, instead of doing what will make them feel more valuable. This tendency to respond with power to loss of self-value is a remnant of early human history when diminished status meant greater threat to survival. (Lowered status reduced the odds of group protection and reproductive opportunities.) Although such threats to survival are minimal now, adults who habitually react in the Toddler brain perceive a similar threat in minor ego offenses. When offended, many simply don't know how to make themselves feel valuable. The only option apparent to them is exerting power, either overtly (through criticism or aggression) or by mentally devaluing people around them.

Of course, adults in the Toddler brain devalue others more skillfully than real toddlers, often concealing their retaliatory impulse with amazing deftness. One popular way of devaluing people these days is by "diagnosing" them with emotional or personality disorders. A cottage industry exists to encourage us to do just that, featuring symptom checklists associated with personality disorders. Some books and blogs are written by advocates or "survivors," who describe how you should react to your partner, coworkers, and bosses using words of contempt, such as "congenitally manipulative, opportunistic, cunning, exploitive, wolf in sheep's clothing, sociopath, psychopath." Others are written by therapists who psychoanalyze your coworkers, bosses, and partners with various explanations of why they make you feel bad. Both types of fast-food diagnoses describe the insidious behavior of their favorite personality disorder, not so much to inform and enlighten as to appeal to the reader's impulse to feel morally superior to the diagnosee. These diagnosing books and blogs typically fail to emphasize that a *preponderance* of items on legitimate symptom checklists (most people have a couple of them) must be present, and they must date back to preadolescent developmental stages.

A valid diagnosis is the result of careful, *objective* examination by a trained professional who takes a thorough biological, social, and psychological history, supplemented by psychological testing. Not even trained professionals can validly (or ethically) diagnose family members, current or ex-lovers, and friends. Even physicians are not supposed to diagnose family members, but at least physical illnesses have biological markers. A personality disorder is not something you have, like you can have cancer. It's a description of behavioral tendencies that persist over a lifetime. (Some may have neurological anomalies supporting them, but there is no clear evidence for that as of now.) Of course, validity and accuracy are inaccessible concepts in the Toddler brain. In fact, the descriptions in these books and blogs are little more than stereotypes: women are hysterical and manipulative; men are selfish, exploitative bullies. But in the end, it's not a question of whether the persons we diagnose actually fit the diagnosis. The more important point is that the urge to diagnose keeps us stuck in the Toddler brain, where healing and growth are hardly possible in a torrent of blame, denial, and avoidance.

In the Adult brain, we don't need to diagnose other people to evaluate relationships. All we need is to feel as much compassion and kindness from others as we give and to know that others regard our perspectives as well as we regard theirs. The urge to diagnose is spurred by the Toddler brain seeking power, which impairs the quest for value. Diagnosing others will certainly keep you from soaring above.

When you pathologize anyone, especially an intimate partner, you're bound to destroy what's left of the relationship. But there is a chance to save it if you can reduce emotional reactivity to the person you feel compelled to diagnose. Almost always, the behavioral tendencies that cause pain in relationships are merely Toddler brain habits (which can be replaced by new habits), rather than intransigent personality pathology. Negotiate behavior change in terms of acquiring new habits consistent with deeper values—to replace those sustained by blame, denial, and avoidance. It may not be successful if you've already diagnosed your partner, but at least you'll have a chance of resurrecting the relationship.

Feeling Valuable vs. Feeling Powerful

If you're still wondering about the difference between habits of creating value vs. habits that exert power, consider the following. Basketball players with habits of exerting power are more likely to miss their free throws after being fouled and then foul an opponent shortly after missing the shots. But those in the habit of seeking to feel valuable have tirelessly practiced hitting shots under stress and now focus entirely on draining the free throws. They are more likely to make the shots and less likely to foul an opponent shortly after being fouled. More poignantly, those intimate partners motivated to feel valuable tend to show compassion and kindness to their loved ones. Those moved to feel powerful use deceit or manipulation or invoke shame or fear to get their way, or, in the worst cases, they use coercion or force to dominate.

An Endless Feedback Loop

The human brain must do three operations when confronted with a bad situation. The first is in the Toddler brain. When something bad happens—or seems like it might happen—the alarm sounds in the Toddler brain: fear, anger, shame, anguish. The alarm is usually triggered by *external* change (cues in the environment) or *internal* change—something felt, thought, recalled, or imagined. (Remember, the Toddler brain has only primitive reality-testing; toddlers confuse reality with what they feel, think, remember, and imagine.) The second operation is in the adult brain, where the alarm/signal is interpreted and the perceived bad thing assessed for threat and damage. The third and most important operation, *improve (without making things worse)*, is in the more profound part of the Adult brain. Alas, those who have developed habits of retreating to the Toddler brain under stress tend to get stuck in a feedback loop of the first two operations. Instead of testing the alarm against reality, the interpretations and assessments by habit enhance it by justifying it. They never get to the Adult brain's ability to improve.

Alarm	Interpretation/ Appraisal	Enhanced alarm	Interpretation/ Appraisal	Justification
Fear, anger, shame, anguish, etc.	"I feel bad, confused, depressed, anxious, grieving. Something's threatening or unfair, or someone's doing something wrong."	More anger, shame, fear, anguish.	"It's worse than I thought! It *feels* worse!"	"Of course I feel that way; I have every right to feel that way, after all the bad things that have happened to me."

This unfortunate feedback loop leads us to make the same mistakes over and over. It explains why the manager who needs to increase productivity devalues his employees for not being productive enough. The spouse who wants more closeness criticizes his or her partner for being a selfish failure as an intimate partner. The parent who wants the children to be truthful lies in front of them. The politician who wants to be trusted runs misleading campaign ads.

Keep in mind that getting caught in this Toddler brain feedback loop is just a habit. It's entirely possible, though not easy, to build new habits to regulate the intensity of the alarm automatically (without justifying it) and move quickly into the *soaring* mode. The habit we want to develop in this chapter looks like this:

- Acknowledge the alarm/signal (without confusing it with reality).
- Assess the threat/damage, without blaming, denying, avoiding.
- As quickly as possible, focus on improving.

Reconditioning the Brain

Developing new habits is repetitious and sometimes tedious stuff, requiring factory-like repetitiveness. When I've treated clients on TV shows, the editors had to go through hours of recordings to find the kind of tearful drama they like to show on the air. Oprah Winfrey introduced my first work clients on her show as,

"Thirty hours of intensive, soul-searching therapy." It would have been more accurate to say, "Three hours of intensive soul-searching and twenty-seven of repetitious practice." Her editors had to work so hard to meld together dramatic, tearful footage that I was surprised when she asked me to do another show with different clients.

The mantra for personal healing and growth is: "To get big change, think small." Commit to frequent repetitions of small behaviors to build new habits. The process has an equivalent in physical therapy, where repetitive skeletal-muscular exercises lead eventually to healing and growth. It's also similar to the muscle memory that athletes strive to develop. NBA players may shoot as many as 100 foul shots in practice sessions to get that "feeling in the body" of hitting the foul shots. Three-point specialists take so many practice shots per day that they never have to look for the line in a game; they know in their bodies where it is.

Forming new habits feels really awkward at first. To appreciate how awkward, try this experiment:

Spread your hands as widely as you can, with your fingers extended. Now bring your hands together, with your fingers interlocking. Look at your hands and notice which thumb is on top and which pinkie is on the bottom. Now unclasp them and again spread your arms as widely as possible. Then clasp them together again, with the opposite thumb on top and opposite pinkie on bottom.

Didn't it feel awkward to switch fingers? Here's another simple test. Tomorrow, take whichever shoe you normally tie first, and tie it second. To even have a chance of remembering, you'll need to put a note on your shoes tonight.

If changing such trivial habits like these feels weird, you can imagine how changing entrenched Toddler brain habits will feel. *Don't let the initial awkwardness stop you.* It *has* to feel awkward at first. That's what changing habits is all about! The new behaviors will feel more natural the more you enact them, and they'll eventually become automatic.

Forming New Habits with *TIP*

Most people have entrenched Toddler brain habits of seeking to feel powerful when they get anywhere near vulnerable mental states. The prototype of Adult brain habits is automatically doing something that makes you feel more valuable when you feel vulnerable.

The following are preliminary steps to the all-important practice sessions necessary for developing new habits.

1. Write down, in as much detail as possible, what you thought and felt immediately before the Toddler brain habit was activated, including your physiological states.
2. Identify the antecedents and triggers.
3. Make a list of specific behaviors that make you feel valuable.

Triggers	Antecedents of my bad habits	What I can do to feel valuable
Somebody does or says something that devalues or disrespects me. I remember or imagine something that devalues, disrespects, saddens, or makes me feel guilt or shame.	Hungry, tired, unwell, too much caffeine, alcohol, sugar, sad, lonely, irritable. I'm thinking of how some people take advantage of me or try to control me or disregard me. I'm thinking of ways to get back, to show that I'm smart and capable, and that no one can push me around.	Improve, appreciate, connect, protect. Practice compassion and kindness to people in general.

Once you've completed the above, you're ready to use *TIP*, my method of establishing new habits. The steps of *TIP* are as follows:

- *Think* repeatedly about the desired change and, if you journal, write about it.
- *Imagine* in detail how to overcome any barriers to the desired change.
- *Practice* in simulated stress and in real life the specific behaviors likely to lead to the desired change.

To apply *TIP* to your own Toddler brain habits, practice the behaviors every day for about six weeks. That's the optimal time for building self-regulation habits, although individuals vary in number of repetitions it takes to make a habit. Anything you have to do often works best with a regimen of doing it at the same time every day. If you have trouble sticking to a goal of exercising regularly, it's probably because you try to do it at different times. Practicing at the same time every day establishes a routine whereby you feel not quite right if you don't do it. (The Appendix has a suggested regimen, as well as *TIP* practice logs.)

With practice, you'll replace Toddler brain states of vulnerability—usually shame or anxiety—with more deeply empowering, solution-oriented, Adult brain states. These allow you to act in ways that make you feel consistently more valuable.

Note: I'm using intimate relationships in the following examples. The hardest habits to change are those reinforced by daily routine. Entrenched habits develop naturally, for better or worse, when living with someone, since most of your interactions run on autopilot. If you can change habitual responses in intimate relationships, you can rest assured that *TIP* will help you change any unproductive habit at work.

Desired Change	Thoughts and Writing	Detailed Imagining	Practice
Value more when feeling devalued in my marriage.	When she says that I'm selfish, I'll allow myself to care that she feels hurt and devalued, and I'll let her know that I care.	I feel guilty about having been selfish in the past, but caring about my partner and feeling connected to her is more important, so I will try to focus on what is most important.	I'll ask her to talk about times when she thought I was selfish and practice my more compassionate response.

For a more detailed example of the *TIP* process, I'll use Joel. Like most of my clients, the hardest part of beginning the process was developing a repertoire of valuing behaviors. People who retreat to the Toddler brain under stress simply do not know how to make themselves feel valuable. Remember, valuing behaviors are driven by motivations to improve, appreciate, connect, or protect.

Under *improve*, Joel described how he responded to his boss's rude behavior by recognizing that the company was losing money. He sympathized with his boss, who felt responsible for the losses. Although he couldn't change his boss's behavior, the shift in attitude definitely improved his experience. For *appreciate*, he recalled pulling off the road on his commute to work to watch the sunrise. For *connect*, he wrote about his special efforts to engage with his wife, Marnie, realizing that she sometimes felt isolated due to his natural introversion and, more important, his history of Toddler brain sulking. For *protect*, he remembered spending a Saturday rescuing stray cats for the local pet adoption agency. Once he had these four, he was able to come up with a whole repertoire of valuing behaviors he could do or imagine when he felt devalued.

The Toddler brain habit Joel wanted to change was lashing out at his wife. His anger frightened his wife and kids and made them walk on eggshells, in dread of "setting him off," as Marnie put it. Joel set up his practice sessions to correct this terrible Toddler brain habit by identifying the antecedents, which were almost always tiredness and distraction. He wrote about several times he felt devalued at home. These were mostly small ego offenses, such as Marnie not listening to him when she was busy or when she complained about his not helping with their two kids. The antecedents for him were almost always irritability from sleep deprivation or feeling stressed from deadlines at work; he worked late into the night at a demanding job. Joel imagined that the antecedents and triggers were happening now. He imagined understanding that his tiredness was not Marnie's fault. (If you don't blame irritability on anyone, it doesn't last very long.) He imagined understanding that she was busy and appreciating how hard she works around the house. He imagined protecting her by offering to help with whatever she was doing, and connecting with her through touch or in his imagination, if she was unavailable for touch at that moment. He repeated the association of feeling devalued with the corrective behaviors until it seemed automatic. To simulate the stress of actual interactions, he arranged a couple of practice sessions with Marnie, in which they discussed incidents from the past. Although it lacked the intensity of the actual incidents, the rise in their anxiety from just talking about it was enough to provoke his initial urge to lash out, which he then practiced regulating.

Desired Change	Thoughts and Writing	Detailed Imagining	Practice
Stop the habit of lashing out at Marnie.	When she seems too busy for me, I'll understand that she's busy and appreciate how hard she works around the house.	I'll make some small gesture of connection, a hug or smile or something, and ask if I can help her.	I'll ask her what it is like for her when she's busy and I want attention or when she thinks I'm not helping enough around the house.

Not surprising, daily practice of behaviors like these created more opportunities to improve, appreciate, connect, and protect, making it easier for Joel to become the person and partner he most wanted to be.

Effort Brings Reward

If it sounds like a lot of work to develop Adult brain habits, it is. But I truly believe that it is the only way to reverse the pervasive effects of Toddler brain habits, which, most of the time, lead to failure and pain.

About twelve years ago I ran into Joel and Marnie in a grocery store, with their third child, Alex, then five years old. Joel told me that he talked often about *TIP* and still used it to reinforce his new habits whenever he felt stress building. While we were chatting, the little boy wandered off and broke into a run when his pursuing mother called him. Joel then used his deeper and louder voice to get the child's attention. Alex immediately ran back to us, with a look of glee on his face. With his arms extended, he looked straight up at his tall father. He opened and closed his hands six times, as if trying to hypnotize, while calling out, "TIP! TIP! TIP! TIP! TIP! TIP!" Joel looked at his son with as much pleasure as I felt pride in my former client. I couldn't help appreciate how this sweet little boy could now live an enjoyable life, free of fear.

Never Stop Learning

Education theorists consider novelty a primary motivator for learning. The joy of learning is apparent in infants and very young children, to whom everything is novel. A study I like to call "Disneyland for Rats" placed listless, elderly lab animals in enriched environments with lots of toys and "interesting" things to learn. The old rats became more active, vital, and alert, with better memories for running mazes. Autopsies revealed dendritic growth that was absent in the rats deprived of enriched environments. In other words, the brains of the learning rats actually grew in their advanced age.

Like rats, humans feel more alive, even in advancing age, when learning, which is the most accessible way to improve. Unlike rats, we can invent our own novelty. An effective way to do this is to develop new habits and skills, while sharpening those old ones that allow us to soar above.

Habits that activate the Adult brain under stress help us develop radical self value, which is the subject of the next chapter.

CHAPTER 10

Radical Self-Value Breeds Radical Value of Others

There are two hard things to do in life. But if you can't do them, you're unlikely to be successful at work and will have practically no chance of enjoying a satisfying intimate relationship. The first is holding on to self-value when you don't like other people's behavior, so you don't feel devalued by it. The second—impossible to achieve if you don't master the first—is holding on to value for other people when you don't like their behavior, so you don't devalue them because of it.

Obviously, feeling devalued and devaluing others will make any situation worse. The problem of holding on to to self-value goes beyond the fact that the Toddler brain typically dominates under stress. A complicating factor is the inflated notion of *self-esteem* that has emerged in the public consciousness in recent decades.

Not coincidentally, the Culture of Toddlerhood is also the age of high self-esteem. The general population currently scores higher on self-esteem measures than any that came before it. Some researchers have identified a decidedly upward trend in narcissism, which is an inflated sense of one's talents, skills, and personal qualities, with a strong sense of entitlement to high regard from others, special considerations, and rewards of all kinds.

Self-esteem, as traditionally measured, is how we feel about ourselves in comparison to others. But as people experience it, self-esteem tends to have a hierarchical bias. That is, we're better than some and, by implication, not as good as others. Self-esteem also has a dark side, as noted in the research of Roy Baumeister and colleagues, summarized in the book *Evil: Inside Human Violence and Cruelty*. Baumeister observed that high self-esteem is often fragile and subject to abrupt and painful deflation when the rest of the world demonstrates that it doesn't feel as good about those who have it as they feel about themselves. Worse, when the world does not meet their entitlement expectations, many with high self-esteem feel wronged and, therefore, justified to retaliate with manipulation, abuse, or violence.

The hierarchical bias of self-esteem traps many people in the Toddler brain, where it seems that they need to feel better than someone else to feel okay about themselves. Not surprisingly, hierarchical self-esteem lies at the heart of racism, sexism, and all other prejudicial points of view. A particularly abusive form of this unfortunate way of looking at the self and the world is *predatory self-esteem*. To feel good about themselves, persons with predatory self-esteem need to make other people feel bad. They're critical, controlling, demanding, hard to please, and often domineering or abusive. You may have worked for a predator in your first job. (They can rise to low-level supervisory jobs before shooting themselves in the foot.) These are people who seem to get off by putting down everyone around them. They like to make you feel stupid for not already knowing the job they're supposed to be training you to do.

While they're a scourge to work with, the predators' usual victims are members of their own families. Many family abusers test high in self-esteem, while everyone else in the family tests low. The predator will not stay in treatment, of course, since all the family's problems are someone else's fault. So when intervention increases the self-value of the emotionally beaten-down spouse and children, who will then no longer internalize the put downs, the predator's self-esteem plummets. Predators can feel okay only when they make others feel inferior.

A less repulsive but still unpleasant variation of hierarchical self-esteem is *self-righteousness*. People who disagree with the self-righteous are worse than "wrong," they're "immoral!" Those who don't keep house the way they like it have no idea how "decent" people should live. If you don't meet their whims, you're selfish and unworthy, if not condemned by God.

You will never see a person with hierarchical, much less self-righteous or predatory self-esteem, lead a meaningful, balanced, or satisfying life. That's because it's not possible just to look down on people. The very structure of hierarchy condemns you to look up as much as you look down. Whatever criteria you use to judge superiority (they're all arbitrary), you'll meet plenty of people with a lot more of it than you. You will meet a whole lot of folks who are smarter, stronger, richer, more powerful, better looking, more popular, with greater spirituality or keener sensitivity, or who wear better socks. Failure is the inevitable end of this self-destructive notion of personal value.

Hierarchical self-esteem is self-defeating because it requires at least an implicit devaluing of others. When we devalue someone else, we devalue ourselves; our sense of well-being deteriorates, we violate our basic humanity to some degree, and we become more narrow and rigid in perspective to justify the devaluing. When we devalue someone else, we experience a devalued state wherein the drive to create value becomes less important than the will to control or dominate (or at least be seen as right). Devaluing others locks us in the Toddler brain and guarantees that we'll get Toddler brain responses from others.

The impulse to devalue always signals a diminished sense of self. That's why it's so hard to put someone down when you feel really good (your value investment is high) and equally hard to build yourself up when you feel resentful. (As Khalil Gibran said, "To belittle you have to be little.") Think of things you say to yourself and others when resentful: "I shouldn't have to put up with this," "I deserve better," "Just look at all the good things I do." When you value others, that is, when your self-value is high, you don't think of what you have to put up with, and you certainly don't feel the need to list the good things you do. Rather, when confronted with life challenges, you shift automatically into improve mode: you try to make bad situations better.

It's often hard to notice that we're in devalued states, because devaluing others requires a certain amount of adrenaline to overcome humane inhibitions. The adrenaline creates a temporary feeling of power and certainty. Remember, adrenaline makes you feel like you can do anything, as long as it stays in your bloodstream. (I believe this false confidence from low-grade adrenaline is the reason that some people with low self-value score high on self-esteem tests.) But the confidence lasts only as long as the arousal lasts. To stay "right," they have to stay aroused, negative, and narrow in perspective: "Every time I think of him I get pissed!"

Devaluing others never puts us in touch with the most important things about us and, therefore, never raises self-value. On the contrary, its whole purpose is to make someone else's value seem lower than our own. If it works, we're both down; if it doesn't, we end up lower than where we started. In either case, personal self-value remains low and dependent on downward comparison to those we devalue, creating a chronic state of powerlessness. The motivation to gain temporary feelings of power by devaluing others occurs more and more frequently, until it takes over everyday life.

Self-value is more behavioral than emotional, more about how we treat ourselves than how we feel about ourselves in comparison to others. To value goes beyond feeling that the valued persons or objects are important; you also appreciate their qualities, while investing time, energy, effort, and sacrifice in their nurturing or maintenance. If you value a da Vinci painting, you focus on its beauty and design more than the cracks in the aged paint. Above all, you treat it well, making sure that it's maintained in ideal conditions of temperature and humidity and shielded from direct lighting. Similarly, people with high self-value appreciate their better qualities (while trying to improve their lesser ones) and take care of their physical and psychological health, growth, and development.

Where self-esteem is hierarchical, self-value is about equality. If you believe in the essential equality of all people, based on your most humane of values, you'll never meet anyone superior to you. A steady supply of well-being comes from efforts to increase other people's self-value by treating them without regard to talents, station, or status, and with dignity and respect. The royal road to self-value begins with value of others. Think of how you feel when you're loving and supportive to those you love, compared to when you devalue them. When we value someone else, we experience more vitality, meaning, and purpose. Valuing others makes self-value soar.

I've spent my career training people to do something that will make them feel more valuable when they feel devalued. This unique Adult brain activity is the only real protection from the fragile sense of self that results from Toddler brain reactivity (when the inability to control how other people think, feel, and behave makes us feel devalued). The secret lies in the word "valuable"—able to value. To feel valuable, we must value. If everyone's self-esteem were higher, there would be even more conflict and violence in the world. But if everyone's self-*value* were higher, the world would be a better place.

In general, the more we value other people, animals, and things, the stronger self-value grows; the more we devalue, the lower self-value sinks, making Toddler brain coping mechanisms seem necessary. Chronic resentment, anger, substance abuse, impulsive behavior, or abuse of others are all self-destructive signs of low self-value, although they may well signal high self-esteem. A radical approach to self-value makes these and other maladaptive ego defenses unnecessary.

Physical Well-Being

The first aspect of radical self-value is commitment to make your physical health important and worthy of appreciation, time, energy, and sacrifice. Begin by reading some of the plethora of information about wellness, diet, and exercise, and then decide what is optimal for you. Pursue your regimen of health vigorously, not only for yourself, but to make the world a better place.

Emotional Well-Being

The second aspect of radical self-value is commitment to make your emotional well-being worthy of appreciation, time, energy, and sacrifice. Emotional well-being has many dimensions. Following are the major ones.

Acting on What Is Most Important

If you've read this far, you won't be surprised to learn that the most potent contributor to consistent emotional well-being is fidelity to your deepest values. When true to our deepest values, we feel more genuine. When we violate them, we experience guilt, shame, and anxiety, not as punishments, but as motivation to be authentic.

Much of the suffering in the world occurs when people violate what is most important to them by acting on what is less important. If you think of the big mistakes you've made in life, nearly every one involves violating a deeper value by acting on something that was not *as* important to you, at least in the long run.

We consistently violate more important values by acting on less important feelings and impulses. We're susceptible to this recurring error for two reasons. Deeper values do not run on automatic pilot like habits and impulses. Processed in the brain in milliseconds, habits and impulses largely bypass the prefrontal cortex, where we make decisions based on values. That's why acting on superficial feelings, which are largely Toddler brain responses, usually makes us violate deeper values. Don't focus so much on how you feel; instead, focus on what you value.

Surveying the Environment

We continually survey the environment for objects of attraction and threat—food, affiliation, sex, saber-toothed tigers, and snakes in the grass, as one evolutionary anthropologist put it. Some people continually survey the environment for anything that might possibly be negative. They have trained their brains, quite inadvertently, to look for things that will make them feel down, resentful, anxious, or angry, which they inevitably find and almost always blame on the people around them.

The Adult brain can learn to do the opposite: look for something to appreciate. Although it takes practice to build a habit of appreciating, the reward is nothing short of radical self-value. There are innumerable things in the environment that can stimulate interest, curiosity, enjoyment, courage, compassion, and kindness. Multiple studies have shown that whatever the brain looks for, it will find, for better or worse. Radical self-value makes us look for the better.

Benign Interpretations

As we've seen, a primary function of the Adult brain is to interpret and explain both our internal experience—what we think and feel—and our perceptions of the world around us. With radical self-value, we give our experience the *most benign interpretations realistically possible*. I don't mean mere positive thinking or putting on rose-colored glasses; these are really Toddler brain solutions to complex problems. The Adult brain analyzes the complexity of problems to choose the more benign interpretation when the evidence for either is more or less equal. For instance, an interpretation dominated by Toddler brain alarms might regard media coverage as evidence that the world is a dangerous place, rife with crime and violence. The Adult brain, seeking to learn more about what triggers the alarm, discovers that violent crime is actually on a rather steep decline, despite sensational news coverage that distorts reality by focusing on one small part of it. This more realistic interpretation frees us to focus more on the small acts of compassion and kindness we see in the course of every day, while taking care to avoid high-risk situations. In other words, we'll notice people holding doors for strangers and giving help when needed, while avoiding dark alleys with hundred-dollar bills hanging out of our pockets. We should never ignore Toddler brain alarms in assessments of reality, but we should never confuse them with reality or allow them to inhibit Adult brain assessments that lead to the most long-term growth and well-being.

Soaring Above Pain

To soar above is to go beyond limits, to become greater, to become the most empowered and humane persons we can be. This, I believe, is the evolved function of pain: not to suffer or to identify with suffering but to grow beyond it. As we've seen, the natural function of pain is to motivate behavior that will heal, correct, and improve. The Adult brain uses pain as fuel for growth.

Create Value When Devalued

When we feel devalued, we must do something that will make us feel more valuable, not more powerful. Creating value under stress is a simple but transformative skill that anyone can acquire with practice, as outlined in Chapter 9.

Try this experiment: The next time you feel powerless or devalued, do something that makes you feel more valuable (e.g., something that reflects compassion or kindness). In about twenty minutes (shorter, if not a lot of cortisol was secreted with the negative emotion), your self-value will be higher than it was *before* the powerless feeling occurred. You'll like the feeling of self-value so much that you'll want to practice the skill until it begins to occur automatically.

Holding On to Value for Others Under Stress

You may have figured out by now that holding on to value for others under stress follows from holding on to self-value. Stress makes many of us retreat to the Toddler brain, where self-obsession and splitting compel us to look for someone to blame. Because this is an entrenched habit, it takes a new habit to replace it. Use the *TIP* process (Chapter 9) to form habits of improving, appreciating, connecting, or protecting when under stress. These will automatically activate the Adult brain, where radical self-value will give you the ability to soar above.

Developing radical self-value contributes enormously to personal happiness, but it is by no means sufficient to that end. To be truly happy, you have to try, in some small way, to make the world a better place, as we'll see in the next chapter.

CHAPTER 11

How to Be Happy
Make the World a Little Better

It's all too ironic. In our Culture of Toddlerhood, what people ultimately feel entitled to is happiness. Yet happiness is simply impossible when self-obsession is the norm and other people are deemed worthy only insofar as they agree with us or validate how we feel. We fall prey to this cruel irony because the Toddler brain struggle for autonomy makes us lose sight of our inexorable interconnectedness. In reality, we cannot make ourselves happier without striving, in some small way, to make the world around us a little better.

If you doubt that your personal well-being is related to your desire to make the world better, as I'm sure many readers do, try this mental exercise. Pretend that when you woke up this morning, you felt the value and importance of everyone in your household. (You probably believe they're all valuable, but you don't often *feel* it, especially first thing in the morning. But you're imagining that on this morning you did feel it.) When you left the house, you regarded all your neighbors as important and valuable people. Driving to work, there were no jerks on the road; everyone was a good and valuable person. You arrived at work to meet a collection of good and valuable people.

You get the picture. If you had actually valued and respected everyone you saw today—just in your head, without overtly changing your behavior at all—how would you feel right now? And if you regarded everyone you saw with value and respect, would that make it more or less likely that they would regard the people *they* encountered with value and respect? That's right, you would have spread value and respect throughout the community, making the world a little better place.

Now suppose you woke up and found things to resent about the people you live with. Some of your neighbors were complaining about your lawn and some weren't taking in their trash cans. You saw only jerks on the drive to work. And when you got there, it seemed like people were talking about you behind your back. If you regarded everyone you saw with suspicion or mistrust or just ignored them because they weren't worth your attention, how would you feel right now? And if you devalued the people you encountered, would that make it more or less likely that they would devalue the people they meet?

Happiness That Lasts

The Adult brain transforms the self-obsession that precludes lasting happiness into mature *self-awareness*. The difference is that Adult brain self-awareness necessarily includes awareness of the world in which the self resides.

Self-awareness has been considered a virtue since the time of Socrates, who declared that the unexamined life isn't worth living. Lao-Tzu told us, "At the center of your being you have the answer; you know who you are and you know what you want." Shakespeare instructed us, "To thine own self be true." Carl Jung informed us, "Everything that irritates us about others can lead us to an understanding of ourselves."

In our own time, research links self-awareness—but not self-obsession—to psychological *and* physical well-being. In general, the self-aware feel better, do better, and enjoy better health. Self-awareness guides our behavior and provides correction messages when we make the wrong choices. For instance, my client Frank reverted to his Toddler brain this morning when he was about to berate his assistant for making a mistake. Just in time, he shifted back to his Adult brain by remembering that he felt like yelling at her only because he wants to yell at himself when he makes mistakes. The correction message generated by self-awareness helped him focus on improving the conditions her mistake caused, without wasting time and energy on railing about how much trouble the mistake created, as he would have done in the past. Showing value and respect for his assistant helped them both be more productive and significantly happier.

The truly self-aware know intuitively that enduring happiness—
that which surpasses temporary feeling states—comes from striving, in some small way, to make the environment they live in a
little better. All animals have a drive to make their environment
better, although in regard to other animals, "better" just means
safer, more comfortable, or pleasurable. Those things are important but clearly not enough for humans. We want the world to be
fairer and more moral.

"Better," whether applied to comfort or values, is a relative term,
sometimes confused with "great" or "good." Because we cannot
make the world we live in great or good, we often lose sight of the
deep desire we all have to make it better. Feeding that desire helps
us grow. Ignoring it keeps us locked in the Toddler brain.

To Make a Big Change, Think Small

Fortunately, even the smallest ways of making the world better
can be powerful, by virtue of the *butterfly effect*. In chaos theory,
the butterfly effect holds that the smallest change in one part of
the ecosystem affects large changes in other parts. The classic met-
aphor has a butterfly flapping its wings in one part of the world,
setting off an extremely complex chain of events that results in a
hurricane on the other side of the globe. Although not as glamor-
ous as its ecological cousin, social psychology has its own simpler
version of the butterfly effect. In human experience, the butterfly
effect is powered by the most fundamental instruments of interaction and cooperation: modeling, emotional display, and mimicry.

Modeling is the primary way that young animals, including humans, learn to negotiate the world they live in. Adults model the behavior that the juveniles mimic. (Sorry if you are still under the illusion that your children learn from what you tell them. In fact, they learn emotion regulation and other kinds of self-control from watching you.) Modeling occurs both actively and passively. In its active form, it's simply exhibiting the behavior the modeler wants others to adopt. I'm diligent and passionate on the job when I want my employees to be diligent and motivated. In its grander form, modeling invokes the Golden Rule of doing unto others as you would have them do unto you. I'm respectful to you when I want you to be respectful to me. Conversely, passive modeling inadvertently exhibits behaviors you don't want others to adopt. I can't expect my children to tell the truth when they catch me lying. Neither can I expect to be valued by others when I criticize everyone I see. And from the bottom up, how reasonable is it to expect an honest government when we cheat on our taxes?

Although evidence of the power of modeling is copious in animals, we underestimate its global influence on human behavior. The reason we universally condemn hypocrisy—indeed, are repulsed by it and consider it a form of betrayal—is due to its violation of the implicit trust we place in modeling.

All animals, including humans, use *emotional display* to interact with one another. Aggression is the most dramatic example. Dogs growl, cats arch their backs, snakes hiss, horses stand tall and thrust their front legs forward, bulls kick sand, gorillas beat their chests, and humans puff up their muscles. (Early humans used to bellow and screech, which is why we talk in a more resonant and menacing voice when angry and want to scream in traffic.) There are just as obvious though less dramatic gestures of courtship, affiliation, interest, and playfulness. In humans, emotional display has social and cultural "rules" that define the appropriateness and acceptability of when, where, and how emotions are expressed. Displays acceptable in a funeral home would be deemed inappropriate in a movie theater.

The aspect of emotional display most common in the butterfly effect is made up of the nonlinguistic manifestations of emotions, predominantly facial expressions, body language, and tone of voice. This is how we "get a feel" for each other. The feel we get for each other forms the basis for how we regard others and how we interact with them. Brain imaging suggests that we make initial judgments about people before they say anything. "Good morning" can be interpreted as cheerful, if we're predisposed that way, or we can deem it sarcastic, if that's our predisposition before we interpret the words.

In biology, *mimicry* occurs when one species takes on the characteristics of another. In reference to social animals, it means adopting, usually without conscious awareness, behavior modeled by others. The recent discovery of mirror neurons in monkeys suggests a neurological basis for mimicry. These nerve cells in the brain fire when the monkey does something and watches someone else do something, creating an impulse to mimic. The evidence for mirror neurons is more speculative in humans at this time, but our propensity for mimicry in social contexts is not. We rely on mimicry for social order in more subtle ways than seem apparent. Mimicry provides predictability, cooperation, and a sense of safety in social contexts. In addition, social norms require that people mimic behavior deemed appropriate. The force of mimicry is most noticeable in its violation, as when someone shouts, sings, or disrobes in a restaurant.

Widespread mimicry is apparent in studies of behavior in social settings, ranging from mirroring body language and facial expressions to parroting speech and adopting uncharacteristic behavior, like laughing at things in a group that you don't find funny when by yourself. You've probably noticed that couples who live together a long time begin to look like each other, due to each mimicking the other's facial expressions and body language. Mimicry even approaches something like a swarming effect in moving crowds. Swarming has been traditionally associated with insects, birds, and fish, but not humans. An amusing example of the human swarming effect occurs when subway passengers exiting the train in rush hour follow a couple of graduate students in a less direct path to the escalator than they would have chosen on their own.

For Personal Happiness, *Model* Improve, Appreciate, Connect, Protect

In general, active modeling is an Adult brain activity, while mimicry begins in the earliest socialization of the Toddler brain. If we don't actively model what we want from others, we'll most likely mimic what we don't want by reacting in the Toddler brain.

If I do not show respect for you, I'll likely mimic your disrespectful behavior. Toddler brain reactivity virtually guarantees a vicious feedback loop that ultimately turns us into the very thing we despise. Think of how often you've seen people exhibit the very behaviors they condemn in others, including criticizing those who criticize. Liars are outraged by liars, the rude cannot abide rudeness in others, and the self-righteous ridicule that tendency in their neighbors. We become intolerant of the intolerant, resentful when around resentful people, and abusive when abused. In the extreme, virtually all abusers and criminals perceive themselves to have been abused or exploited at some point in their lives, though usually not by those they abuse and exploit in the present.

You may have noticed that personal happiness does not come from criticizing or from focusing on what you don't want others to do. But we *can* be happier by focusing on what we want to model and by practicing the behaviors we want others to mimic. You can see this for yourself by making a list of behaviors and attitudes to model for the next three weeks. To gain the full benefit of the experiment, choose behaviors and attitudes from the *value motivations* discussed in Chapter 8: improve, appreciate, connect, protect. I'll review them briefly.

Improve

Human beings have a drive to improve. We function at our best when trying to improve and begin to lose meaning, purpose, health, and well-being when we stop trying to improve. Remember that *improve* means striving to make something *a little better*, not necessarily 100 percent better. Think of improving as an incremental process—making things a little better at a time.

Protect

Protection of valued persons is a fundamental survival instinct. We are not descended from the early humans who lacked the instinct to protect and, as a result, went extinct. The elements of protection are to:

- Nurture
- Reassure
- Encourage
- Support
- Show love and affection.

Think of ways you have done these and ways you will do them in the future.

Appreciate

We live in an era of sensory and information overload. Lost in the glare of gross information and hyper stimulation is the transcendent emotional state of appreciation. Even though we have a great deal more to appreciate, with far less daily hardship and suffering than most of our ancestors, people report that they experience relatively little appreciation in their lives.

Appreciation requires opening your heart and allowing yourself to be enhanced by the experience of someone or something. In the act of appreciation, life means more to us.

Remember John F. Kennedy's admonition to "never forget that the highest appreciation is not to utter the words, but to live by them."

Connect

It's ironic that in our era of mass social media and instant electronic access, so many of us feel disconnected. A recent survey revealed that 62 percent of American adults have talked to no one or to only one person about anything important to them in the last six months. A Harvard Medical School study describes loneliness as "a very real and little-discussed social epidemic with frightening consequences." For a multitude of people, social media has become more of a distraction than a vehicle of connection. Constant distraction has deepened the void of meaningful connection that digital media was supposed to fill and made us more aware of how disconnected we truly are.

The types of connection are:

- Basic humanity—compassion, kindness
- Familial—emotional resonance with kin
- Intimate—personal well-being intertwined with that of another
- Spiritual—relating to something larger than the self
- Communal—identifying with a group of people, based on shared values, goals, or experiences.

Example of Modeling Improve, Appreciate, Connect, Protect

Herb was the head of a team working to close a huge commercial real estate deal that was worth tens of millions of dollars. Near the closing, two team members botched a filing that could cost the firm several millions in taxes and attorneys' fees. Without blaming, Herb marshaled everyone's efforts to build in another revenue stream on the property to make up for the loss. He made a point of appreciating how hard the team was working. Although he didn't express it directly, his appreciation elevated the mood of the entire team. He urged everyone to bring pictures of their families into the conference room. Just the symbolic presence of their family connections got everyone to work harder. He reassured and encouraged them. At the end of the day, the pair responsible for the misfiling found a way of developing storage space on the property. Amortized, the total would more than compensate for the loss their mistake would incur.

Stand for Something

If we're not good for something, we'll be good for nothing.

When I was in the Cub Scouts, we stood for things such as "honesty, loyalty, justice, and fair play." And we all knew that Superman stood for "Truth, Justice, and the American Way." It was cool to stand for something then, although we had no idea what the phrase actually meant.

The coolness of standing for something changed in the mid-1960s, when we "discovered" that what we'd been told to stand for was someone else's values—"the Man's," we called it. "The Man's" values led to mindless conformity, empty materialism, class struggle, and war. So we embarked on a drug culture that separated feeling good from doing good. Not surprisingly, standing for something remains out of favor in the Age of Entitlement. Now we have even more intellectual conformity (with *thought police* tirelessly enforcing political correctness); more empty materialism (households have many times more clothes, devices, beauty aids, gadgets, and cars than those of the 1960s); more, though less dramatic, class struggle (due to greater diversity of population and inequality of resource distribution); and more war (wars are far more frequent, albeit on smaller scales). Our judgments and behavior generally derive from feelings and short-term self-interest rather than values, even though we know that behavior motivated by feelings and by pure self-interest rarely produces long-term well-being. Now, more than ever, we need a paraphrase of Thoreau's famous admonition, "Feel not simply good, feel good for something."

Standing for something requires conviction, a strong belief that a behavior is right, moral, and consistent with your deeper values. Like Toddler brain resentment, Adult brain conviction provides a sense of confidence about what we believe and do. The crucial difference is that the confidence of conviction is likely to endure across all moods and frames of mind, whereas self-doubt returns as soon as the intensity of resentment fades.

Sometimes it's easy to confuse conviction with resentment, as both provide motivation and energy. The best way to know that you're acting out of conviction and not resentment is to state *why* your behavior is right, moral, and consistent with your deeper values. If your answer has conviction, it will represent your deeper values. For example, I did not press charges when a student stole an expensive device from my office. I chose instead to teach him Adult brain skills to resist Toddler brain impulses, which I knew he would not learn in jail.* In contrast, explanations of resentment-driven behavior inflate the ego or devalue someone else. For example, Raphael decided to have no further contact with his family because they weren't as educated as he.

Here's a more complex example of the difference. Theo knew that he was right to take the children and leave his alcoholic wife, who was harming them emotionally. He continued to regard her compassionately and support her the best he could, but he had to put the well-being of their children first. That's what he stood for.

The path to conviction was not easy for Theo. It was clear from the start that he was bound in what I call a "pendulum of pain." Resentment would pull him away from his wife, until the distance between them grew to the critical point of actual separation. Then, like clockwork, the shame of his perceived failure as a husband and guilt over what would happen to his wife if he left swung him back toward her. But resentment almost always blocks emotional

---

* I'm not presuming that this would be the right choice for everyone. Having had counseling experience in the criminal justice system, it was right for what I personally stood for.

connection. His continuing resentment about her drinking would soon get the pendulum moving back in the opposite direction, until it once again reached the critical point of separation, where it would swing back toward her. This constant pendulum swing, between nearly leaving on the one end and failing to reconnect on the other, had gone on for nearly seven years before I met him. What finally gave him the strength to take the kids and leave was his hard work in treatment to develop conviction that he was acting on his deepest value—protecting his children—by leaving. As it turned out, his bold action prompted his wife to seek professional help for her drinking. After a couple of relapses—typical of addiction treatment—she was able to maintain sobriety. More important, she was able to get back in touch with what *she* stood for—loving and nurturing motherhood. The family was reunited.

When you act out of conviction, you might be disappointed or saddened by the outcome of specific behaviors or negotiations, but you'll be far less likely to regret your behavior. Theo felt sad when he left his wife, and that would have lasted a long time had she not overcome her addiction. But he never would have regretted leaving for what he stood for: protecting their children. On the other hand, had he left her out of resentment, he would have devalued her to justify his decision. That would have made the separation harder on the children, which would have caused him still more guilt, shame, and regret.

"For" vs. "Against"

An important feature of conviction is that it's *for* something—for example, the well-being of loved ones, justice, fair treatment, or equality—while resentment is *against* something: mistreatment of loved ones, injustice, or unfairness. The distinction may seem subtle, but it's crucial to healing and growth. Those who hate injustice want retribution and triumph, not fairness. They fantasize about punishment of their unjust opponents, who stir "justifiable" contempt. If Theo had left his wife out of resentment, he most likely would have developed contempt for her and covered up his guilt with fantasies of punishment: "She got what she deserved!" This would have harmed their children and alienated him from his core value.

Just as it's sometimes difficult to distinguish resentment from conviction as a motivator, a gray area seems to exist between the more intense versions of these states, namely anger and passion. In general, Toddler brain anger becomes passion in the Adult brain. The crucial difference is that passion is value-oriented, where anger is devaluing. The former is for something, like justice, while the latter is against something. The fantasies of those who love justice are of equality, harmony, and triumphant good, while the fantasies of those who hate injustice include inflicting humiliation or punishment on perceived offenders. Being *for* something creates positive feelings of interest, passion, or joy, which improve health and relationships. Being *against* something foments negative feelings of anger, contempt, envy, or disgust, which have deleterious effects on health and relationships.

Organizations that stand for something turn out to be more effective than those that do not. In the book *Firms of Endearment: How World-Class Companies Profit from Passion and Purpose*, business school professor Raj Sisosda analyzes a collection of companies that outperformed their peers over a fifteen-year period. Much of what separates the brands of conviction from the competition is their commitment beyond profit-seeking to a sense of purpose in making the world a little better.

Three-Week Experiment

The best way to reduce the Toddler brain vulnerability that so often leads to self-defeating behavior is to strengthen who you are, what you believe in, and what you stand for. Begin your experiment by listing five things you stand for, the things that are most important to you and worthy of your time, energy, and sacrifice (examples: fairness, hard work, honesty, compassion, kindness):

1. _____

2. _____

3. _____

4. _____

5. _____

For the next three weeks, adopt all the things you listed above as motivations, guides, and measures of all your behavior. If you feel irritated, bored, resentful, or angry, redouble your efforts to embody what you stand for. To the extent that you're successful, you'll notice substantial improvement in feelings of authenticity and well-being. Paraphrasing Thoreau, "You won't just be good, you'll be good for something."

Regret Prevention: Establish a Legacy

After a quarter-century of clinical work and research with highly distressed families, I regard my practice as the business of preventing regret. Any therapist who has worked at all with mentally intact seniors will tell you that a palpable regret is the strongest thing they see in their offices. According to research and clinical experience, people regret choices about education, work, and, most profoundly, failings in close relationships—as partners, parents, siblings, and adult children.

It serves us well at any age to take time out occasionally to think of what we might regret in the future. Now is the time—the only time—to prevent regret. And the best way to start is to consider your legacy: what you want to leave behind and what you want to contribute to humanity.

The most tragic regret that people suffer near the end of their lives is that they have not been more compassionate, loving, and supportive to those they love. You've likely had a presage of this kind of regret if you've experienced the untimely death of a loved one. The common self-doubt, even in relationships that were very close and loving, is something like the following:

- "Did she really know how much I loved her?"
- "Did I make him understand how important he was to me?"

The first step toward avoiding the ultimate regret is to review the following questions about deeper values, most of which were presented earlier in the book.

- What is the most important thing about you as a person?
- What do you want those you love to think about you?
- How do you want your loved ones to feel about you?
- What kind of relationships do you want your children to have in school, in work, in love?
- Are you modeling for your children the relationships you want them to have?
- What would your life mean to you if you lost your family?
- Near the end of your life, what might you regret the most?
- What do you want to contribute to humanity?

If answering these questions still seems hard, the second step in preventing regret is even more difficult. Behaviors that lead to long-term regret tend to be habits and, therefore, resistant to change through insight and desire alone. Changing habits entails forging new habits incompatible with those you want to change. Use the *TIP* process from Chapter 9 to build habits that are consistent with the way you would like to answer the above questions. For example, if you think you'll regret not being affectionate to your spouse, it's not enough to make a resolution to be more affectionate. That's just talking the talk. If you want change that endures, use *TIP* to build habits of expressing affection. Do it now, before it's too late.

In summary, lasting happiness, emotional well-being, physical health, and personal attractiveness depend to a large extent on how we regard others, which, in turn, determines how we interact with them. In short, the way we regard other people determines how we experience life. Every time you regard someone positively, you make your life better, and every time you disrespect or ignore someone, you devalue your experience of life.

The Golden Promise

If you focus continually on making the world a better place in some small way by improving, appreciating, connecting, and protecting, you'll develop conviction, stand for something, and model those things for other people. In a small way, you'll make the world a better place. You and those you love will be happier, your life will have more meaning and purpose, and you'll create a legacy that will give you peace in your later years.

There are millions of things you can do to make the world better in a small way. From a psychological point of view, *what* you choose to do is less important than the choice to do something with the goal of making the world a little better. The secret is to think small and give the butterfly effect a chance to work on the Web of Emotion, which we'll take on in the next chapter.

CHAPTER 12

The Adult Brain in the Web of Emotion

Everything We Do Makes the World Better or Worse

We saw earlier how emotion contagion and reciprocity influence interactions among people. Unless we self-regulate, angry people make us angry, sad people make us sad, and irritable people make us irritable. Happy people tend to cheer us up, although reciprocity and contagion work less forcefully with the positive, due to the negative bias of emotions.

The principles of emotion interaction work on a more subtle level as well. All social animals, including humans, put out subtle emotional signals, most of which are outside conscious awareness. Like all social animals, we can pretty much *feel* when someone is putting out positive or negative emotional energy, even if he or she commits no overt behavior. Although we can't tell what they're thinking, we can read the emotional tone of most people with a fair degree of accuracy, whether they're quiet, brooding, anxious, resentful, or shouting. How many times have you asked someone, "Is anything wrong?"

"No, nothing's wrong," was the response. You didn't buy it because you *felt* there *was* something wrong.

Even when we consciously try to shut out our subtle sensing of one another, we retain our natural sensitivity to each other's emotions. That's why you feel different when you ignore your spouse compared to the way you feel when he or she is not in the room with you. It's why you feel different when you're the only one walking down the street compared to how you feel when the sidewalk is crowded with people, whom you try to ignore.

The Web of Emotion

Compelling evidence from a variety of scientific disciplines shows that we automatically and continuously synchronize with the facial expressions, voices, postures, movements, and emotional displays of others. This automatic emotional reactivity occurs in milliseconds and is thus well outside conscious awareness. The milliseconds our brains take to process emotional tone is much faster than the formulation of thoughts, beliefs, and values. That is to say, we react to emotional tones emitted by others that have little to do with who they really are as people, and so we do not see them.

Our innate sensitivity to one another's emotional states derives from the social nature of the central nervous system. From the beginning of our time on this planet, humans lived in groups and tribes and communicated, in prelinguistic times, by transmission of emotions. We are very much social animals, hardwired to interact emotionally, in subtle yet profound ways, with *everyone* we encounter.

On a deep, visceral level, we continually draw small bits of energy from—and contribute small bits of energy to—a dynamic Web of Emotion that consists of everyone we interact with and everyone with whom they interact. Each person you pass on the street subtly reacts to you and vice versa. Everyone you pass by subtly influences each person he or she passes. In the Web of Emotion, you never react to just one person but to everyone that person has recently passed by, and your influence on them holds in a small way with everyone they will subsequently encounter. Whether we like it or not, we're emotionally connected to virtually everyone we perceive. Our only choice is to make the connection positive or negative, to put out compassion or pick up resentment, to clean up emotional pollution or contribute to it.

Web Sensitivity

Try these three experiments to test your sensitivity to the Web of Emotion.

1. The next time you're in a meeting or with a group of people, try to note the "feel" of the group, whether it's subtly positive or negative.

2. Walk down a moderately busy sidewalk and note the emotional tone of passersby. Try to notice the subtle *approach modes* (friendliness), *avoid modes* (ignoring you), and *attack modes* (superior, devaluing, or looking down on others). You should notice that the vast majority of those you pass are in *avoid modes*, which you might experience as a slight chilliness or even rejection. Some will be in *approach* mode, and now and then you'll find someone in *attack* mode. Note your reactions to each.

3. Try to influence the Web of Emotion. As you pass each person on the street, think that he or she is a valuable and important person. But you can't just *think* positively; you have to *feel* in your heart that *everyone* you pass is a valuable person, worthy of respect and appreciation, and that every person is capable of love and compassion. (Appreciate that the vast majority of the people you see would share their last bit of water with a desperate child in a desert. This image creates a basic humanity connection with other people that helps you soar above.) Note your feeling after a block or two of doing this.

The Vast Contagion of the Web of Emotion

It takes some preparation, but the following is a fascinating experiment to try. With the secret cooperation of a friend, record a video of a group of five or more of your friends filling out a longish form. Don't tell them why they're doing it; just say it's an experiment. (You probably have friends who will agree to do this for a lark. It really is fun.) After about ten minutes, your secret collaborator should display some *very subtle* signs of resentment. The goal is to bring out unconscious contagion, so it can't be obvious. At regular intervals, a couple of minutes apart, your undercover friend should:

- Tap his pencil on the desk, as if impatient with the form
- Give a barely audible sigh
- Turn the page with a slight rustle of the corner.

After about five more minutes, the people on either side of your secret plant will begin to do the same kind of behavior. Then the ones sitting next to those two will start. On average, this little joke gets 40 to 60 percent of the participants doing miniature displays of resentment as they fill out whatever forms you gave them.*

Now here's the kicker. When they're finished with the forms, ask the friends who showed subtle resentment if they got a little irritated

---

*It's not the length of the forms that causes the resentment; it's the staged resentment of the secret collaborator. I've tried it without a plant, using the same forms, and found no signs of resentment.

or resentful filling them out. Some will have no idea what you're talking about. Others will claim to have felt nothing at all. They will be surprised when you show them the recording of their resentful behavior, which they had done completely outside their awareness.

Resentment is the most contagious state in the Web of Emotion, due to its subtlety. More overt displays of anger are repulsive, but resentment seeps in under the radar. Though often invisible, its contagious effects are everywhere.

General and Continuous

Even in its lowest grade of intensity, resentment is a *general* nervous system arousal. That means it generalizes itself; if you're resentful at one person, you are less likely to be nice to another. Rather than a defense against a particular offense, resentment is a defensive *system* that is active much of the time, flowing continuously back and forth from work to home. If your spouse says something you don't like as you're leaving the house, you'll probably drive aggressively and be less pleasant to coworkers or schoolmates when you get to your destination. If something seems unfair at work or school, you're likely to drive aggressively and not be as sweet to your kids when you get home. Or things can be going just fine at home and work, until a jerk on the road stirs resentment that washes into the other venues of your life, causing you to inject still more negative energy into the Web of Emotion. This happens to only a few of us all the time, but it happens to all of us some of the time.

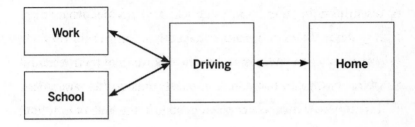

Common Enemy Bonding

Resentment in the Web of Emotion facilitates a kind of social bonding called "common enemy." People used to form emotional bonds by mutual values. We were more likely to care about one another if the same things were important to us. Examples are church, school, and professional communities. Today we are more likely to bond if we resent the same things: "You don't like the president? I don't either!" Now more than ever we subscribe to the proverb, "The enemy of my enemy is my friend."

Common enemy bonding—us against them—is the most primitive, superficial, and weakest kind of emotional bonding. Toddlers do it on a miniature level in play groups. It emerges more strongly on playgrounds when one child is made an "out girl," so that the others can bond over resentment of her. As children mature and begin to cluster in groups, one group will make outcasts of another, forming clubs, cliques, and gangs. The adage "Politics makes strange bedfellows" expresses the common enemy syndrome when otherwise incompatible factions join together in opposition to a policy or program. The Allies prevailed in World

War II due to the unlikely union of capitalism and communism against a more loathsome common enemy.

Whether on the playground, in Congress, or on the world stage, common enemy bonding is sure to fall apart as soon as the external threat diminishes. If the school bully moves away, the union against him falls apart. We saw the Cold War envelop Europe as soon as the hot one ended. The ethnically diverse populations of the old Yugoslavia held together in part because of the Soviet threat. Once the Soviet Union ceased to exist, the people of various ethnic factions suddenly remembered how much they used to hate each other, even though most of them were not alive during earlier versions of those hostilities.

We occasionally try to use the common enemy effect to mobilize "attacks" on social, economic, and personal problems. Thus we've had various "wars" on drugs, poverty, crime, and inflation. The predictable failure of these efforts owes to the inability to extract blame from resentment. Sustained resentment at a common enemy requires demonization of *persons*, not abstract economic or social phenomena. So we retaliate against those who take drugs, suffer poverty, or commit crimes. We build more prisons, admonish the easiest scapegoats, and lose interest as soon as we can't figure out who's to blame for more complicated circumstances. Resentment in the Web of Emotion can lead only to the simplest and least appropriate solutions to complex social, economic, and political problems.

Beware of forming bonds with individuals or groups because you dislike the same people or resent the same things. The trick, once again, is to focus on what you are *for* rather than what you're *against.* Say that an organization against domestic violence keeps its focus on everything that it devalues. Its members motivate themselves with anger and resentment, which they inevitably turn on one another. Such places are notorious for complaints, infighting, backstabbing, and sabotage; they are unpleasant places to work. Advocacy groups motivated by resentment tend to multiply like rabbits without increasing their membership. Disagreements within the groups splinter them into smaller and smaller units, competing with each other for media attention and community resources. The message of the cause becomes secondary to the competition for advancing it. But an organization *for* something— like safe, respectful relationships—keeps the focus on everything it values. Its members are motivated by passion for what is right— what they stand for—rather than resentment about what is wrong. Such organizations enjoy more cohesion and cooperation, and are simply more pleasant places to work. Bond over what you stand for, not what you're against. The latter inevitably leads to resentment and aggression, which you'll automatically transmit to others via the Web of Emotion.

Resentment and Aggression

Suppose you're driving down the road at a baseline level of arousal, that is, with no resentment or anger of any kind. Suddenly an obnoxious event occurs, like someone flipping you the finger and shouting something about your mother as they speed by your car. If you're at baseline to begin with, that might get you about 30 percent aroused, which is no big deal. Your response will likely get no worse than sarcasm; you'll think, *What a jerk*, or maybe even shout something back at him. That kind of anger dissipates in a few minutes and is forgotten about completely within a couple of hours. You're not likely to remember it ever happened.

But if you get into the car resentful about something going on at home or at work, you're already about 20 to 30 percent aroused at the start. So that same obnoxious event isn't hitting you at baseline. You're starting out partially aroused and are more likely to reach a 60 to 70 percent arousal level. That's where you begin to get aggressive, with a hair-trigger mechanism for escalation, should there be any negative response to your aggression. Add caffeine, anxiety, or a startle response to the mix, and the adrenaline can easily go through the roof. This kind of anger will stay with you in various degrees for the whole day, and you'll get pissed every time you think of the incident.

Aggressive Driving in the Web of Emotion

My agency, CompassionPower, has offered court-ordered classes to people arrested for aggressive driving violations in Maryland and Virginia. Our work there has yielded evidence of the Web of Emotion at work on our roads and highways. By way of background, incidents of aggressive driving are more likely to occur if the driver is resentful about something. Of course, Toddler brain impulsivity and entitlement make aggressive drivers regard the road as theirs, giving them the "right" to drive any way they want. But there's a more subtle aspect to the relationship of resentment with aggressive driving. Resentment is a low-grade form of anger. All anger prepares the organism for one purpose and one purpose only: to fight. The physical and mental changes that occur with resentment impair judgment and deteriorate fine motor skills; you're more likely to be impulsive and do things like turn the wheel too hard when resentful. Your eyes dilate slightly, increasing peripheral vision at the cost of depth perception, because early human predators used to attack from the side, never from the front. In other words, you become less accurate at judging distances, which explains why so many resentful drivers tailgate and cut off other motorists; they're actually closer than they perceive. Resentment degrades judgment and slows reaction time. Due to the increased blood flow to the muscles during any kind of anger arousal, you are likely to drive faster than normal. It doesn't take much of an increase in blood flow to make the foot a little heavier on the gas.

If you doubt the effects of resentment on your driving, try this experiment. The next time you drive at the speed limit on the highway, try to think of some occurrence at work or home that stirs your resentment. Think about how unfair it is and how you deserve better treatment—how it *should* be this way or *shouldn't* be that way. After a minute or so, look down at the speedometer. You'll notice that you're going fifteen to twenty miles per hour above the speed limit. If the traffic doesn't allow so big an increase in speed, you are likely to be tailgating, with an impulse to change lanes abruptly.

All right, you get the picture that resentment can cause aggressive driving, but how does that prove the effects of the Web of Emotion? A survey of people who were court-ordered to take our aggressive driving course showed that nearly 80 percent of them were caught responding in kind to being cut off, tailgated, or screamed at by other drivers. Because it was done to them, they felt justified in doing it to someone else—a classic response of Toddler brain resentment.

There's also a peculiar anonymity to driving. We respond emotionally to *vehicles* rather than anonymous drivers whom we can't see through tinted windows or hear with our radios blaring. Because vehicles are not *personal*, you can play out your Toddler brain reactivity on *any* of them, not necessarily the one that offended you, much like a toddler pulling the ear of the dog because Mommy said "No" to a request for a cookie. So an SUV might cut you off, but you're likely to tailgate or speed by the first car that gets in your way because it feels like you have the right. You were offended, damn it, why should you have to wait in line, too? Resentment makes you feel like a victim, which seems to justify almost any kind of lashing-out retaliation.

In regard to the Web of Emotion, the most aggressive behavior on the road is not cutting someone off or tailgating, although these are certainly dangerous things to do. In terms of the maximal effects, leaning on the horn when someone else drives badly is by far the most insidious. The loud noise of sustained horn blowing increases the arousal level of *everyone* near you, not just the jerk you want to punish. The jerk may have made you mad and more likely to drive aggressively, but you have done the same to every driver who was startled by your horn blast and every Toddler brain driver they pass down the road.

Wait, it gets worse. I was asked to develop an aggressive driving program a few years ago. I knew that the core of the program would be emotion regulation techniques based on core values, which I had developed for family violence offenders. Since we already had a large database of graduates of that program, I suggested that the Maryland Motor Vehicle Administration (MVA) analyze a sample of our graduates' driving records. They randomly selected 300 graduates of those who were court-ordered to attend family violence classes. Their analysis uncovered a surprisingly strong link between aggressive driving and family violence. Fully two-thirds of the family violence offenders had multiple aggressive driving violations in the year before treatment. These are violations like tailgating, running red lights and stop signs, and unsafe lane changes—impossible to detect without the coincidental presence of a police officer. Yet the average number of convictions for these offenses by the family violence offenders was 3.4 in *one* year. By normal estimates of the number of infractions versus the number of times getting caught, these people were driving aggressively virtually all the time. Of course, some of the resentment that fueled their aggression started at home and went onto the road, but since most of the infractions occurred in the afternoon rush hours, a lot of it was starting at work or on the road going home. A great many of the incidents of domestic violence and child abuse our clients reported started within an hour of arriving home from a stressful commute. The aggression these drivers bring home with them is exacerbated by the fact that so many of them reach for a drink or two or three once they get there, just to "unwind."

Another finding in the Maryland MVA analysis that pertains to the Web of Emotion was that CompassionPower's family violence intervention, which never mentioned driving, reduced these aggressive violations by 98 percent in the year following treatment. This was *three times better* than a matched group of drivers ordered into standard driver improvement classes, which focused on driving skill but did not address resentment, anger, or aggression. Our classes managed to greatly reduce aggressive driving by shrinking the baseline resentment levels of our clients. The classes spent a lot of time teaching emotion regulation skill, which helped clients shift from the Toddler brain to the Adult brain, where they were less likely to drive aggressively. Our graduates were not only driving less aggressively, they reported less resentment and strife at work, while 86 percent of them were free of violence one year following treatment, based on reports of the spouse or child victim's social worker.

The good news here is that stricter enforcement of traffic laws, which require classes in impulse control and emotion regulation as a consequence of violations, may reduce family violence. Conversely, raising other people's resentment on the road can lead to abuse in untold households. The *great* news is that being nice to the people you meet, even jerks on the road, may help prevent child abuse. By virtue of the Web of Emotion, we can protect the safety and well-being of every other driver on the road and that of their families and coworkers off the road.

Remember the mirror test in Chapter 4. The world does not see the unfairness, hurt, or betrayal you feel inside; it sees only your resentment, which seems unfriendly, rejecting, or even mean. In the Web of Emotion, other people react only to what they see on the outside. To change the way people react to you, you must change the way you feel, which means activating your core value motivation to improve, appreciate, connect, or protect whenever you feel resentful. The stakes couldn't be higher. If you do not try to spread compassion and well-being in the Web of Emotion, you will most certainly let in streams of resentment, putting yourself and everyone you encounter on a path to misery.

The next chapter shows how to build a web of compassion, kindness, and love.

CHAPTER 13

To Soar Above, Build a Web of Compassion and Kindness

Compassion is the antitoxin of the soul:
where there is compassion even the most poisonous
impulses remain relatively harmless.

—ERIC HOFFER

No isolation is so great as lack of compassion for
others and no emptiness so desolate as lack of compassion
for self. You cannot do a kindness too soon, for
you never know how soon it will be too late.

—RALPH WALDO EMERSON

No act of kindness,
no matter how small,
is ever wasted.

—AESOP

There was a man in a plane going down who wrote a five-word note for his family. He put it in a mint tin so it wouldn't burn up in the crash. The charred note read, "Be nice to each other."

Another man, trapped in a collapsed coal mine, wrote to his family as the oxygen left the small cavity where he lay: "It wasn't so bad, I just went to sleep."

Think of the many phone messages that came out of the burning towers on 9/11. No one spoke of resentment or contempt or hatred or revenge, only compassion and kindness.

The borders of our lives, if they are to make sense, must be compassion and kindness.

Compassion and Survival

The survival of human beings on this planet owes more to our sense of compassion than our propensity for aggression. Early humans had to prevail against more powerful and plentiful predators, against whom our intelligence alone would have had met with little success. Just look at what we were up against. Our chief competitors, big cats and wolves, cranked out a couple of litters a year, while our human ancestors had one offspring at a time, with very high rates of miscarriage and infant mortality. In addition to being outnumbered, the physical limitations of early humans put them at a severe disadvantage in the survival sweepstakes. They lacked claws, sharp teeth, speed, agility, and strength. They could not see, smell, hear, jump, or climb trees as well as more powerful predators. They couldn't see at all in the dark, while big cats were nocturnal hunters. In this precarious environment, the ability to form tightly knit social units to hunt and fight collectively was crucial for survival. One person against a saber-toothed tiger had no chance, but five fighting together would prevail.

Two things must be present in a psychological system that consistently overrides the choice for individual survival. There has to be a strong motivation to get people to risk their lives for others in the first place and a powerful reinforcement to keep them doing it once they experience how dangerous it is.

The powerful motivation that got early humans to risk their lives for others in the tribe was probably a form of *psychological merging*. It had to seem to the rescuers like their *own* lives were at stake, as if their own existence would end if they did not help endangered brothers and sisters. Interviews with modern heroes give a clue as to how this motivation to put one's own life at risk might have been experienced. Modern heroes—police officers, firefighters, military personnel—often say that they could not conceive of *failing* to rescue. It seemed to them like a force greater than their fear made them do it. I heard a firsthand account of this many years ago when I interviewed a policeman in his hospital room. He was in traction as a result of grabbing a man who was trying to jump off a bridge. He held the man with one arm while leaning over the balustrade, his head almost parallel with the top of the ice-cold railing. Help didn't come for nearly twenty minutes. I asked whether in all that time he considered letting go of this man who, after all, was trying to commit suicide. His reply: "It felt like if I let go, we'd both die."

For our early ancestors, the force of psychological merging under intense stress had to overcome threats to their individual lives. Those tribal members whose genes had a compassionate and cooperative tendency passed on those genes, while those who did not, perished. In those perilous times of early human history, rescuing fellows in danger could not be just a one-shot deal, for there was always another saber-toothed tiger around the bend. There had to be rich internal *and* social rewards—reinforcement both within and without—to *keep* people risking their lives for one another. These bountiful rewards were and *are* in the Adult brain—an enhanced sense of self and a general feeling of self-value for compassionate and cooperative behavior. The person who defended a child against attack by a predator probably felt *great* about himself afterward. And that high self-estimation was sure to gain social reinforcement, as fellow tribespeople admired his courage or regarded her as a hero. Yet positive reward wasn't always enough to ensure survival of the species. There had to be harsh punishments for failing at compassion. A person who cowered behind a rock while a child succumbed to a predator would suffer severe guilt and shame and probably abandonment anxiety. If the tribe found out about it, the coward would face derision, if not banishment to a certain death by starvation or predator.

So the reward for compassionate behavior was as good as it could get: pride, self-value, well-being, and social admiration. And the punishment for failure of compassion was as bad as it could get: guilt, shame, self-loathing, social derision, and fear of abandonment. These potent rewards and punishments for group loyalty drive human interactions in everything from primitive tribal affiliation to complex community and national identities. Think of the pride of being "American" or "Christian" or "Jewish" or "Muslim," compared to the guilt and shame of being disloyal to one's affiliations. Identification with a group has traditionally provided us with a sense of safety, security, emotional connection, and value. Disloyalty to groups has brought rejection, banishment, and death.

The motivation to help fellow tribesmen began as a life-or-death instinct in early humans. It evolved into the life force that now drives us to create connections of value. The human instinct to be compassionate is what we think of as our humanity; we judge people to be lovable if they are compassionate and to be inhumane if they are not. More important, we judge ourselves according to our level of compassion, no matter how much we may delude ourselves with inflated egos or try to blame, deny, and avoid our way out of it. Consistent failure to be compassionate eventually yields self-loathing.

Justifying Failure of Compassion

The strongest argument for the instinct to be compassionate is the fact that we have to justify failing at it. Thus we have concepts like the "worthy poor"—a classification supposedly linked to those physically or mentally unable to help themselves. (By implication, the rest of the poor are "unworthy.") This kind of rationalization gives us a way to live with ourselves while failing to act on our natural instincts for compassionate behavior. How many times have you heard someone say, "Why should I care about them?" or "What about *me*?" They're arguing with themselves, with their own instinct to care and to help.

Soar Above the Threat of Compassion

People know intuitively that successful relationships require a certain amount of compassion. Yet some people become so invested in justifying their resentment and toddler coping mechanisms that they begin to view compassion as the cause of their hurt. They fear (and ultimately shrink from) the better angels of their nature.

Much of the dread that blocks the most healing and bonding of human emotions comes from confusing it with lesser experience, specifically:

- Pity
- Agreement

- Excusing bad behavior
- Trust
- Manipulation

Thank God that we can shine the light of the Adult brain on these unfortunate and unnecessary impediments to soaring above.

Compassion vs. Pity

Compassion implies equality: "I sympathize with your hurt. Despite our differences in luck or circumstance, we're (humanely) equal." Pity implies inequality: "I feel sorry for you because you're incompetent, naive, insensitive, crazy, abusive, or defective in some way." Compassion is caring about the well-being of another. Pity is feeling bad at the sight of another's suffering. This particular feeling of inadequacy quickly turns to contempt, as we blame the dysphoric feeling on the person stimulating it. Bertolt Brecht mused that the first time we see a beggar on the street, we'll pity him. The second time, we'll call a policeman to have him removed.

Adults in the Toddler brain often confuse autonomy with acting morally or intellectually superior, only to be surprised by the negative reactions to what they think is compassionate behavior. Their presumption of inequality—"I feel sorry for you because you're incompetent, crazy, abusive, or personality disordered"—will make any sympathetic behavior come off as pity. To a large extent, pity is the opposite side of the coin from contempt. That's why we hate to feel pitied but long for compassion. *You cannot be genuinely compassionate if you believe you're superior in any way.*

When heartfelt compassionate acts garner a negative response, you can bet that the behavior, however sincere, was construed as pity. In the Toddler brain, compassion often feels like pity, and pity often passes for compassion. In the Adult brain, compassion is transcendent, freeing us from the prison of self-obsession. We soar above by caring more, not by pretending to be superior.

Compassion vs. Agreement

Compassion requires sympathy with the pain or discomfort of another, regardless of agreement about beliefs or ideas. You can disagree with ideas and behavior and still sympathize with the pain or hardship that may result from the ideas or behavior. Toddlers can't do this because their sense of autonomy is too insecure to tolerate disagreement. Adults in the Toddler brain can't do it because disagreement, especially from loved ones, strikes at both sides of the Grand Human Contradiction. In their autonomy struggle, they feel less in control of their own thoughts and feelings when others don't think they're "right." On the connection side, disagreement feels like rejection; when "inflicted" by loved ones, it feels like betrayal.

In the Adult brain I can disagree totally with someone's interpretation of my behavior or the intentions behind it and still feel compassion for the hardship they suffer because of their misinterpretation. As an added bonus, showing care for the hardship will alter the misperception, while a defensive reaction to it will make it stronger. For example, a woman I nearly brushed—but did not touch—at a crowded concert called after me, "You're very rude!" I recognized that she felt devalued by what she thought was a deliberate attempt to push her aside.

"I'm so sorry," I said. "Are you okay? I was pushed by the crowd behind me and I must have leaned into you. I'm so sorry."

She appreciated my care, which convinced her that, if it *was* I who pushed her, it *was* entirely accidental. Now, had I said, "I didn't push you. There's a big crowd here. Everybody's bumping and pushing," she would have been convinced that I pushed her on purpose. But regardless of her interpretation, I felt better about myself experiencing compassion than I would have felt getting caught up in Toddler brain reactivity.

Compassion vs. Taking Advantage

In the Toddler brain, compassion can feel like you're being tricked, as if someone was hurt or distressed just to take advantage of you. Feeling taken advantage of is loathsome for most people, but that can't happen when you do what you believe in your heart is right. When you act according to your deepest values, you cannot be exploited, even if others violate their deeper values by trying to exploit you.

Compassion vs. Excusing Bad or Irresponsible Behavior

Compassion doesn't condone or excuse bad behavior, because it's not about behavior at all. Rather, compassion focuses on the pain, hardship, and human frailty that make people behave badly, while recognizing that the continuation of bad or irresponsible

behavior will hurt them more. For example, it's not compassionate to give an alcoholic a drink. The worst thing you can do for
an abusive person is excuse the abuse, which contributes to the
abuser's self-loathing (bubbling beneath the inflated ego) caused
by the continual violation of his or her deepest values. Neither is
it compassionate to allow children to behave irresponsibly, lest
they painfully learn later in life how cruel the world can be to the
irresponsible.

Compassion vs. Trust

We never get hurt by too much compassion, but we're hurt all
the time by unwise trust. Compassion makes you less likely to trust
unwisely. With compassion you see the depth of other people's
vulnerability and can more intelligently assess his or her defenses
against it, which are usually resentment, anger, or some kind of
abuse. Compassion must be unconditional in love relationships,
but trust has to be earned, especially once it's betrayed. Compassion gives a couple room to earn trust by disabling the automatic
defense system that takes over resentful relationships.

The Healing Emotion

If it is genuine, no emotional experience can heal like compassion. To deeply understand the hurt of another is to heal your own.

No psychological wound can heal without compassion for self
and for at least one other person. Research firmly supports the
role of compassion as a predictor of success in psychotherapy.
Therapists never *heal* clients; they model compassion for them to

emulate. When the client can experience compassion for self and others, psychological healing occurs.

Apart from therapy, studies show that the support of friends and loved ones is crucial in coping with life's harsher stressors, including sickness and death. Compassionate physicians enjoy a 30 percent better cure rate than those who may be more skilled but less caring. Controlling for the severity of the illness, people in intensive care units with no visitors suffer a lower recovery rate than those who have frequent visitors. Research aside, we have always known the role of compassion in physical healing. What is the first thing you do when a friend or loved one is ill? Call or visit them, ask if you can help, or send a get-well card, flowers, fruit, or candy. Nearly every hospital in the world has a gift or flower shop. Compassion proves to the sick that they are worthy of healing.

Droughts and Floods of Compassion

A traumatic event occurring on a national scale triggers floods of compassion from all over the country. All you see on TV after an earthquake or a school shooting is people reaching out, hugging, caring, and trying to help. Following the horror of 9/11, volunteer work and contributions to charities increased sharply all over the country, while violent crime, aggressive driving, and family abuse declined just as sharply. For a while, we were more important to one another. On smaller scales, you see the same impulse to reach out to one another at funerals. After a terrible fight with your spouse or child, you very much want to kiss and make up. You want to heal the rift, reinstate connection, and make things right. This desire lurks beneath most of the resentment and contempt between partners. It's what keeps them together in the face of continuing pain, even when they don't know how to reconnect. The focal point of all my workshops with highly distressed couples is to get them back in touch with their deep, though heavily defended, desire to be compassionate and kind to each other, which is the only way to dissipate chronic resentment and contempt in close relationships.

A flood of compassion after suffering derives from the survival importance of emotional connection. Under threat we pull together and care more about one another. But just like floods in nature, floods of compassion are unsustainable. They dry up with amazing rapidity. You may have received flowers after a fight with your husband, but that wave of goodwill almost immediately receded into a vast sea of routine. Within days of a death in the family, some of its members are likely to stop comforting one another and start bickering over property or mementoes. Just seven months after 9/11, violent crime, aggressive driving, and family violence had exceeded the levels of September 10, 2001.

Droughts in nature eventually *cause* floods by destroying the topsoil and vegetation that would otherwise absorb rain. So do droughts of compassion create many of the traumas that bring about floods of pain and distress. Lack of compassion on the part of anyone in the home practically guarantees emotional, if not physical, aggression, which will bring about yet another short-lived flood of remorse and caring. (In some cases the drought/flood dynamic turns into a cycle of violence.) None of the known mass killers gave or received sufficient compassion before they committed their crimes. They felt like outcasts and misfits, which was part of their motivation to exact their awful retribution.

Kindness

On the other side of the compassion coin we find kindness. Where compassion is sympathy for—and motivation to relieve—suffering and hardship, kindness is concern for the well-being of others, with a motivation to help them achieve it. Put another way, compassion is about suffering; kindness is about happiness. Important relationships cannot survive without compassion, and they cannot thrive without kindness.

Though it has enormous positive effects on those who give it, compassion, activated by apparent suffering or hardship, has a relatively minor influence on routine interaction with the Web of Emotion, where suffering and hardship are not usually apparent. Kindness is more amenable to the dynamics of the Web of Emotion. Thoughts of happiness and well-being for everyone you encounter will not only spread kindness along the Web of Emotion, it will make you soar above Toddler brain reactivity and self-obsession.

A Steady Trickle of Kindness

When Jan's kid sister died of a drug overdose at age twenty-five, Jan's husband, Roy, stepped up to the plate. "He was a prince," Jan said, her eyes welling as she described that sad time of her life. Roy handled all the arrangements, gave her all the emotional support she could hope for, and was there for her family in every way possible. He got her through the crisis, and she was eternally grateful. But it was neither his flood of compassion nor her gratitude that made their relationship stronger for the rest of their lives.

Although she certainly appreciated the wave of support her husband had provided after the traumatic death of her young sister, what Jan found more endearing was the fact that, some fifteen years later, Roy continued to write her a daily note: "Take care, I love you." He never left the house or came into it without hugging her. Every day, he either brought her a single flower or lit a candle for her. As wonderful as his wave of compassion during the crisis period of her loss was, the small, continuing acts of kindness had more lasting effects on her emotional well-being . . . and on his. He told me that he could no longer be happy without doing these small acts of kindness. Jan was convinced that her periods of "feeling down" were much fewer and farther between because of Roy's small acts of kindness.

Great waves of compassion motivate beneficial behavior but do not sustain it. It's small acts of kindness that provide a *maintenance* level of well-being. We have to feel kindness or compassion at least a few minutes a day, preferably spread out over the course of the day, for optimal functioning. But I can hear many readers asking themselves, *How can I live my life that way? Won't people take advantage of me?* Trust me, you'll prefer living your life that way once you get into the habit, and, no, most people won't take advantage of you. But even if some do, it won't matter, because you'll act out of conviction that you're doing the right thing. In other words, you'll still soar above.

The reason you're not likely to get a negative response to genuine compassion and kindness is what I call the "compassion/kindness paradox." There's a weird paradox about kindness and compassion. If available whenever needed, they're *rarely* needed. Research shows that when people feel secure in the knowledge that compassion and support will be there when they need it, they are far more independent. Worry that it *won't* be available if needed creates *deprivation motivation*, which makes them want all they can get while they can get it, because it may never again be available. Applying *preventive* kindness in small doses, rather than unsustainable floods of compassion after something bad happens, will actually prevent bad things from happening in your relationships.

Compassion and Kindness Make Us Happier, Smarter, and More Attractive

Roy was onto something when he said that he couldn't be happy without doing his small acts of kindness. Brain imaging studies show that pleasure centers in the brain are as equally active when we observe someone giving money to charity as when someone gives us money. In the Adult brain, giving to others increases well-being more than buying yourself something.

Compassion and kindness make us smarter by breaking the self-obsession of the Toddler brain that keeps out vast amounts of information. Compassion and kindness increase our knowledge about—and deepen our understanding of—the people with whom we share this planet. And that in turn makes us more attractive. According to research, people rate kindness as one of their most desired qualities in a potential romantic partner.

True Compassion and Kindness Support Autonomy

Empowerment means helping people gain the confidence to solve their problems. It does not mean solving problems for them. Whenever we do something for another person or a community or another nation, compassion and kindness require that it contribute to their sense of competence, dignity, and long-term autonomy. Kindness and compassion are not mere indulgence in joy or sympathy. They carry a responsibility to promote, at least in a small way, the best interests of others. Because autonomy is so important to the emotional well-being of human beings, compassionate and kind behavior must support the increasing self-sufficiency of the recipient. They function best as a jump start of another's self-compassion, self-nurturing, self-healing, competence, growth, creativity, and compassion for others. The empowering gift of self-sufficiency always underlies compassionate and kind behavior.

A young child wakes up screaming about monsters coming out of the wall. His nurturing parents run to give him comfort. "Mommy and Daddy are here. It's okay. It was just a bad dream.

We'll protect you." They remain a comforting presence until the child falls back to sleep.

However nice this seems, it's not enough. Having performed this initial comforting gesture, compassionate and kind parents go an extra step. "Honey, you were having a bad dream. Then you woke up, half asleep, and saw what looked like something moving on the wall. I can see how, when it's dark, and you're half asleep, it could look like a monster. But now that you're fully awake and the lights are on and Mommy and Daddy are here, let's go over and see what we can tell about the wall."

"Okay," the comforted child says. They walk over to the wall, where the parent points to something.

"What do you think that is?" the parent asks.

"Shadows," the child says.

"Where are they coming from?"

"The leaves from the tree outside the window."

"When the wind blows, they move. I can see how it could look like a monster when you're half asleep. Isn't it funny how our brains can play tricks on us?"

This child has learned not only that his parents are there if he needs them but that *he* has the power to regulate intense feelings like fear by testing their reality.

Defense

Because they are Adult brain experiences, compassion and kindness offer the strongest possible protection from the worst kind of emotional pain: betrayed trust. As strange as it might seem, compassion and kindness makes us *less likely* to trust unwisely, as they provide deeper understanding of the frailties of those who are unable to regulate their core hurts without hurting others. As you become better able to discern when people are in the Toddler brain, it will be easier to tell when they're manipulating, misleading, or trying to take advantage.

My primary example of the protection from unwise trust afforded by compassion and kindness comes from the work I've done in prisons. Some years ago we began an anger regulation group with multiple murderers. (Our hypothesis—that teaching violent criminals to create more value would make them more compassionate and thereby reduce crime—wasn't exactly setting the state government afire with support. They'd let us test it only on a group of prisoners who would never again be free.) Already serving consecutive life terms, these hapless men had no incentive to refrain from violence against other prisoners. As one of them put it, "So they give me another life sentence, I'll get out in the twenty-third century instead of the twenty-second."

Multiple murderers tend to be in the system from early childhood. Their case files look like small mattresses. As I read page after page of social service reports documenting the terrible things that happened to these men as young children, I couldn't help but develop deep compassion for their terrible suffering. This compassion helped me understand that the hurt these men had suffered was too great; they could not be trusted to regulate their vulnerabilities without hurting other people. When they again feel powerless under stress, they are likely to revert to their habitual form of self-empowerment: violence. The treatment helped them to do well in the highly controlled confines of prisons (it reduced their violence by 72 percent), but in the high-stress, complex world on the outside, they would too often feel powerless and would likely revert to their habits of exerting power over others. Compassion and kindness made this apparent in a way that resentment could not have done. In contrast, the resentment that makes us want to lock them up forever is eventually trumped by the knowledge that it costs about $50,000 a year to support them.

Here's a more mundane example of the defensive virtues of compassion and kindness. Say my angry child calls me a terrible name. Compassion for her protects me from internalizing the insult as meaning that I am devalued or unlovable. Rather, I see that *she* feels devalued or unlovable. With that understanding I help her soothe her hurt with kindness, rather than keep us isolated in our resentment. I have a chance of teaching her respect by modeling it.

Choosing the World We Create

Most experts agree that by and large our brains create reality—not the events that happen around us but the meaning we give to those events. (The clichéd version is, some people make lemonade, while others swallow the bitterness.) In creating the meaning of our reality, we choose among alternative descriptions of what the world is:

- A dark, cold, nameless place, where no one is welcomed
  and no one is missed. There's enough darkness in the
  human heart to engulf the globe.
- A boring, listless, meaningless terrain. When we ignore the
  cries of the heart to improve, appreciate, connect, and protect, the heart goes numb.
- A place of threat and alarm, where there is no respect or
  affection, only attempts to manipulate or dominate. There's
  enough destructiveness in the human heart to create untold
  misery.
- A place of light, promise, and connection, where we tune
  in to our basic humanity and try to understand and sympathize with one another's pain and discomfort. There's
  enough power in the human spirit to light up the world.

How alone and forlorn or listless and uninspired or how safe
and hopeful you perceive the world you live in depends on how
valuable you feel. How valuable you feel depends on how much
value you create. If you don't recognize your inherent core value,
derived from the basic humanity you share with other people, you
will devalue others and provoke retaliation from them—or you'll
withdraw and others will ignore or criticize you, or you'll cling to
someone out of fear of abandonment. You won't be able to balance
the drives for autonomy and connection.

To feel safe, you have to remain true to your deeper values and
your basic humanity, which means valuing those around you. If
you begin with the smallest unit of social interaction, you'll create
a reality of light, promise, and connection.

The Smallest Unit
of Emotional Interaction

The smallest unit of emotional interaction is subtle, low-arousal motivation, which is faintly detectable in body posture, muscle tone, and facial expression. It's typically unconscious and automatic; we're simply not aware that we're transmitting it. Yet it happens automatically whenever we walk by people (or animals), sit near them, or even ignore them. In cities and other congested areas, our unconscious, low-grade emotional response typically includes motivation to *avoid*. This affords a little privacy—a place to be alone with one's thoughts in a crowd of people. The problem is that *avoidance* motivations nearly always stimulate a like response in others, creating a continual and highly contagious state of *emotional disconnection*. States of disconnection necessarily lower compassion, kindness, trust, and cooperation and often raise feelings of inadequacy and isolation. Worse, we misinterpret the smallest unit of emotional response as negative. It feels vaguely uncomfortable. To defend against this perceived negativity, we subtly shut out other people by not processing the sensory and emotional cues they project. To them, this automatic shutout feels vaguely like rejection and creates an impulse in them to reject others.

In truth, the slight rise of marginally uncomfortable feeling carries one simple message: "There is no emotional connection with the person you are now encountering." You then have a choice: *connect* or *avoid*. By default, most of us avoid. And the people we avoid in turn avoid the people they encounter, who then avoid the people they encounter, and so on, with each person in the Web of Emotion passing along *avoid* motivations and the subtle negative emotions that go with them. This chronic low-grade negativity punches tiny holes in our hearts that inevitably fill with resentment or numbness.

The figure below shows how we contaminate the Web of Emotion, with each dot representing subtle negativity.

Negative Web

Positive Change

In the last chapter I asked you to imagine valuing everyone you encountered during the course of the day and then imagine devaluing everyone you encountered. Those two little exercises demonstrate that the way we feel—good and empowered or bad and powerless—is determined by the choice to increase the value of experience in the Adult brain or to decrease it by retreating to the Toddler brain. Your choice, whichever it is, will greatly increase the chances of getting a like vibration in the Web of Emotion.

Here's an example of a choice to value or devalue that you make every time you stop at a traffic light. Think of the last time you were in a hurry and it seemed that the light changed abruptly. In that case, the fact that you *had* to stop felt like *submission*. If it did, you felt powerless and flustered. Not that it's inaccurate to view having to stop as submission. You *were* yielding to a civil power greater than your own. But it is just as accurate to look at it the following way: by stopping at the red light, you ensured the safety of everyone who passed through the intersection, and by way of the Web of Emotion, you contributed to the safety and well-being of the community at large.

If you view stopping at the red light as submission, your Toddler brain will likely empower you with an aggressive impulse. You'll fantasize about running the light or devaluing the person in front of you or the traffic control engineers who are supposed to synchronize the damn lights! Or maybe you turned the negative thinking onto coworkers or loved ones. In any case, this impulse to devalue degrades your contribution to the Web of Emotion. On the other hand, if you see stopping at the red light as protecting the safety and well-being of the community, you enrich your contribution to the Web of Emotion, as you control the value and meaning of your experience.

Remember, if your personal power does not come from creating value and meaning, it will almost certainly come from the Toddler brain—in the form of aggression—either overtly (in someone's face), passively (behind their back), or merely in your imagination. Eventually this will have devastating effects on your emotional well-being, not to mention your relationships and job performance. And it won't just affect you. The negative flow of your unconscious emotions will negatively affect the Web of Emotion. The people you influence negatively will influence others in the same way. All but the occasional Mother Teresa or Buddhist monk will carry that negative reactivity to everyone they encounter; most will take it home to their families.

Now here's the good news about the Web of Emotion: it allows us to influence how compassionate and kind the world becomes. The social design of our brains contains the secret of happiness: influence others to attune to positive emotions. I'm not talking about Pollyannaish good cheer and positive thinking, which, after a while, become cloying and irritating to others. I mean connecting your most humane values to the most humane values of others, with the most subtle of low-grade approach motivation. Here's how.

Imagine that everyone you pass by would rescue and comfort a desperate child. (The few sociopaths who might not do it cannot detract from the billions who would.) Try projecting your most heartfelt basic humanity image onto others. You'll see that connecting your humanity to that of other people will raise your well-being substantially. Become passionate about it, and you will soar above.

Changing the World

You can save the world in a very simple way. Value everyone you see, connect your most humane values to theirs, and then let the principles of modeling, mimicry, emotional display, contagion, and reciprocity do their stuff. You don't even have to make eye contact; *it will work if you only do it in your head.* Just regard everyone you see as a person of value. This creates a very subtle, mostly unconscious approach motivation, to which most people are likely to respond in kind, with subtle positive regard of the people they subsequently pass on the street. Many of the people you value on the street will take that unconscious, low-grade valuing state with them. They're more likely to be nicer to their children and more pleasant to the people they see at work. And so will you.

Value every driver you see, even those who behave badly, and you'll do a great deal to protect the safety of each child and adult with whom you share the road.

This new torrent of transmitting value along the Web of Emotion need not change your overt behavior at all. It will require next to no investment of time and energy. In fact, it will generate energy and give a sense of purpose to your time that might otherwise be empty or wasted. It will help you appreciate a fact that we easily ignore in our rushed and highly structured society: each person you pass on the street is as valuable as anyone in the world.

I value you—a thought to yourself but directed at others—is one of the most powerful statements you can make. In the long run, your contribution to the Web of Emotion will improve family life and help build communities. You will soar above as you make the world a better place. *Every area of your life will improve* if you wake up each morning thinking, *I will spread good in the world today.*

Once we understand that value flows out of us rather than into us, we realize our power to transmit value throughout the world. By virtue of the smallest unit of emotional response, we begin to create the Web of Compassion and Kindness.

Postscript

Here is a log to help you keep track of your positive contributions to the Web of Emotion. You will no doubt notice that when your score on positive contributions is high, you feel better.

Log of Contributions to the Web of Emotion

1 = not much

2 = some

3 = above average

4 = a lot

5 = most of the time

Today I silently regarded each person I encountered as:

Inherently important and valuable   ____

Someone who would rescue a child in a desert   ____

A person who can appreciate a sunset or
    something else in nature   ____

Capable of compassion, kindness, and love   ____

EPILOGUE

I n these pages I have tried to present the importance of employing the Adult brain under stress when those around us are in the Toddler brain. Not only can we reduce the self-obsession and reactivity that run rampant in our time, we can use the most profoundly evolved part of the brain to soar above them.

To soar above is to go beyond limits, to become greater, to become the most authentic and humane adults we can be. This is not a birthright or an entitlement. Rather, it's something we must earn. This epilogue reviews the major points that, when practiced, help us earn the ability to soar above. It goes one step further. But you'll have to wait until the end for that.

The necessary conditions for soaring above are:

- Use pain to grow greater
- Do what makes you feel valuable, rather than temporarily powerful
- Create meaning and purpose
- Balance the Grand Human Contradiction

- Love like an adult
- Use the Web of Emotion to make the world a better place
- Develop a legacy
- Look for the light

Use Pain to Grow Greater

This, I believe, is the evolved function of pain: not to suffer or to identify with suffering or maltreatment, but to grow beyond them. (The natural motivation of pain is to motivate behavior that will heal, correct, and improve.) We don't so much heal emotional injury as outgrow it.

Do What Makes You Feel Valuable, Rather Than Temporarily Powerful

We get stuck in the Toddler brain when we confuse loss of self-value with loss of power. We're then apt to respond with *temporary* feelings of power—anger or resentment—driven by low-grade adrenaline. Most of the time this unfortunate habit leads to further violation of our deeper values and ultimately more feelings of powerlessness. We can and must develop habits of doing what makes us feel more valuable. Whenever we feel devalued, we must increase self-value by improving or appreciating or protecting or connecting (intimately, communally, or spiritually).

The only way to change Toddler brain habits is to override them with new Adult brain habits. Insight and desire do not change habits. Thinking about the desired change, imagining it in detail, and assiduously *practicing* new behaviors—*TIP*—is the path to lasting change.

Create Meaning and Purpose

Try to focus on what you want to *value*, not on how you *feel*. If you act on your values, feelings will eventually follow, as you'll feel more genuine. But acting on feelings will make you violate your deeper values and lead you, sooner rather than later, to feel guilty, ashamed, and phony, with the only available confidence due to the temporary adrenaline-driven illusion embedded in resentment and anger. Fidelity to your deepest, most humane values creates a sense of meaning and purpose. Insofar as feelings enter into choosing behaviors, the emphasis should be on how you *want* to feel. Focusing on how you feel invokes the past; attention to how you want to feel leads to a more meaningful present and future.

Balance the Grand Human Contradiction

In the Adult brain, you feel authentic, with no impulse to struggle for autonomy. You don't dwell on Toddler brain alarms: how bad you might feel and who's to blame. Rather, you think of how to make your situation or your experience of it better. You might feel like sulking or zoning out or getting away from a distressed partner, but the desire to improve, appreciate, protect, and connect is more important than indulging that temporary feeling. Acting on your deeper values makes you feel more autonomous and more connected.

Love Like an Adult

When interactions with anyone you care about start to get stressful, shift into your Adult brain. Focus on how to improve, appreciate, connect, or protect. Strive for binocular vision: the ability to see other people's perspective alongside your own.

Adults in love understand that their only chance of getting the partner they most want to have is to be the partner they most want to be. Learn from your partner how to love him or her, and teach your partner how to love you.

Use the Web of Emotion to Make the World a Better Place

On a visceral level, we continually draw energy from—and contribute energy to—a dynamic Web of Emotion that consists of everyone we interact with and everyone with whom they interact. Whether we like it or not, we're emotionally connected to virtually everyone we encounter on any level. Our only choice is to make the connection positive or negative, to put out compassion or take in resentment, to clean up emotional pollution or contribute to it.

Now the good news: the smallest positive contribution to the Web of Emotion makes the world a little better place. If you focus continually on making the world a better place in this small way, you and those you love will be happier, and your life will have more meaning and purpose.

Develop a Legacy

Now is the time—the only time—to prevent regret. And the best way to start is to consider your legacy—what you want to leave behind, what you want to contribute to humanity.

Look for the Light

Humans have evolved many ways of experiencing and expressing spirituality. From a psychological standpoint, it doesn't matter which way you choose, whether it's some notion of God or a higher power or the cosmos or the sea of humanity or communion with nature. We function at our best with a sense of connection to something larger than the self, something that overrides purely selfish concerns. What all forms of spirituality have in common is a striving to find light.

But light also makes shadows, and shadows fill up with doubt. We must not be afraid of the dark, as we have much to learn from it. When we look deeply into darkness, light begins to reemerge.

Strive every day to look for the light. The ultimate in spiritual experience comes from as bright a light as we can muster from a multitude of sources, creating a supernova of humanity.

The more light we create, the more we soar above.

APPENDIX

Exercise and Logs: Forming Habits That Increase Core Value

I
dentify a repertoire of thoughts and behaviors that make you feel more valuable. These will be practiced in association with your vulnerable states to form beneficial habits. The goal is to automatically do something that will make you feel more valuable when you feel devalued.

Think about times in the past when you felt more valuable. Hint: value-enhancing behaviors tend to fall in four general categories: *improve* (try to make the situation a little better), *appreciate* (open your heart to be enhanced by the qualities of someone or something else), *connect* (attune to your partner's positive emotional experience or deeper vulnerability or isolation if the surface emotion is negative), and *protect* (look out for the emotional well-being of someone else).

Improve example: Most people are able to improve situations in love relationships when they listen to their partners during disagreements. Instead of trying to refute their partners, they provide more information, which tends to make them feel more valuable and their partners feel more valued. The corrective behavior in this example is *listening without contradicting*, which you would practice when feeling devalued.

My improve behaviors:

1. _____
2. _____
3. _____

Appreciation example: My wife stayed up with me all night in the emergency room of the hospital after I suffered a kidney stone attack. The corrective behavior in this example is to *imagine her fighting off exhaustion because she didn't want me to be alone.*

My appreciative behaviors:

1. _____
2. _____
3. _____

Connection example: When people are angry, they are almost always trying to avoid feeling hurt or vulnerable. If you sympathize with your partner's hurt or vulnerability, you will likely experience compassion and a motivation to help, which will make you feel more valuable and your partner feel more valued. The corrective behavior in this example is to *focus on your partner's hurt or vulnerability and try to help, even when he or she is angry at you.*

My connection behaviors:

1. _____
2. _____
3. _____

Protective example: Imagine your response if a stranger said or did the most hurtful thing you have ever said or done to your partner. The corrective behavior in this example is *imagine yourself protecting the well-being of your partner—reassuring, encouraging.*

My protective behaviors:

1. _____
2. _____
3. _____

To develop habits of choosing value over power, use *TIP*:

- *Think* repeatedly about the desired change and, if you journal, write about it (e.g., "When my partner says I'm selfish, I will allow myself to care that he/she is hurt and show that I care").
- *Imagine* in detail how to overcome any barriers (usually guilt, shame, anxiety) to the desired change (e.g., "I feel guilty about having been selfish in the past, but caring about my partner and feeling connected is more important, so I will try to focus on what is most important to me").

- *Practice* in simulated stress and in real life the specific
  behaviors likely to lead to the desired change.

"Practice in simulated stress" means that your partner will
deliberately provoke you with various comments and behaviors
that in the past were followed by angry outbursts, for example,
voicing an intention to buy something desired but not, in your
opinion, "needed." (The practice incidents should be *varied* to
achieve a generalized effect, rather than just desensitize one or
two provocations.)

Set aside three minutes for each practice session. When you're
apart, your partner can text the provocative remarks. After each
practice session, make a mental note of *how much more valuable
the new behavior makes you feel compared to the old response of
anger or aggression.*

Practice associating the "improve, appreciate, connect, protect"
behaviors you described above with feelings of diminished value.
It takes about twelve repetitions per day for about six weeks to
form the new habit.

Anything that has to be practiced that often is more likely to
be accomplished if done in a regimen at the same time every day.
I urge clients to choose transitional times—when we stop doing
one thing and start doing another—to practice the new thoughts
and behaviors; what we experience during transitional times often
has more carryover effect. Each practice session should be about a
minute (three at the most). Using traditional workdays as a model,
practice first thing in the morning, once before leaving the house,

once before going into work, once at morning break time, once at lunchtime, once at afternoon break time, once before leaving work, once before going into the house, once before dinner, once after dinner, once while preparing for bed, once in bed. This regimen works well for most people, but obviously must be adapted to nontraditional workdays and weekends.

* * *

Make a list of the three most recent incidents when you reacted in violation of your core values. Do not provide context or descriptions of the triggers.

1. _____
2. _____
3. _____

Identify the antecedents of the hurtful behavior—what *you* were thinking, feeling, and doing, as well as the state of your physical resources (e.g., hungry, tired, thirsty, having consumed more than two drinks or more than two cups of coffee, or eaten too much sugar) immediately before the infraction. (Don't describe what your partner was thinking, feeling, or doing.)

Antecedent of behavior #1

_____
_____
_____
_____

Antecedent of behavior #2

_____

_____

_____

_____

Antecedent of behavior #3

_____

_____

_____

_____

Practice associating the vulnerable states that led to the unde-
sired behavior with the improve, appreciate, connect, or protect
behaviors you identified above.

Daily Log

Antecedent	Impulse	Corrective Behavior	Number of Times Practiced	Felt Valuable When I Practiced (circle one)
				No Some A lot

ABOUT THE AUTHOR

Steven Stosny, PhD, has treated more than 6,000 people through CompassionPower, the organization he founded and has directed for more than twenty-one years. He is the author of *Living & Loving After Betrayal*, *Love Without Hurt: Turn Your Resentful, Angry, or Emotionally Abusive Relationship into a Compassionate, Loving One*, and, with Pat Love, *How to Improve Your Marriage Without Talking About It*. His textbook, *Treating Attachment Abuse: A Compassionate Approach*, set a new standard for understanding and treating family abuse and was a Behavioral Science Book Selection. His *Psychology Today* blog on relationships is one of the most popular, with more than six million views.

INDEX